JEWISH GERMANY

JEWISH GERMANY

An Enduring Presence from the
Fourth to the Twenty-First Century

DAVID LEVINSON

VALLENTINE MITCHELL
LONDON • CHICAGO, IL

First published in 2018 by Vallentine Mitchell

Catalyst House, 720 Centennial Court
Centennial Park, Elstree
WD6 3SY, UK

814 N. Franklin Street
Chicago
IL 60610, USA

www.vmbooks.com
Copyright © 2018 by David Levinson

British Library Cataloguing in Publication Data:
An entry can be found on request

ISBN 978 1 910383 60 5 (Cloth)
ISBN 978 1 910383 61 2 (Paper)
ISBN 978 1 910383 62 2 (Ebook)

Library of Congress Cataloging in Publication Data
An entry can be found on request

All rights reserved. No part of this publication may be reproduced in any form or by any means, electronic, mechanical, photocopying, reading or otherwise, without the prior permission of Vallentine Mitchell & Co. Ltd.

Printed by Independent Publihers Group, Chicago, IL

Contents

List of Illustrations — vi
Acknowledgements — viii

1. Engaging with Jewish Germany — 1
2. Patterns of Jewish German Life — 7
3. A Quick Historical Tour — 17
4. Uehlfeld's Secret Jewish Past — 31
5. Small Town Life — 50
6. Emancipation and Transformation — 73
7. Freedom and Opportunity — 97
8. City Life — 113
9. City Life – Twentieth Century — 119
10. The Holocaust and New Communities — 127

Appendix: Methods and Sources — 141
Index — 149

List of Ilustrations

1. Artistic Rendering of the New Shul and Old Shul; Fuerth, *c.* 1705. (Courtesy of the Leo Baeck Institute,)
2. An eighteenth-century etching labelled 'Jude' showing a poor Jewish peddler or beggar. (Courtesy of the Leo Baeck Institute,)
3. Gravestones in an older section of the Worms Jewish Cemetery, thought to be the oldest surviving one in Europe.
4. The Uehlfeld cemetery in 1993. Note stones that have repaired or replaced. (Courtesy Hans Gawronski)
5. Uehlfeld Census, 1706.
6. FränkischeDorfjuden, 1817. Oil painting of Jews in rural in 1817. (Courtesy of the Leo Baeck Institute,)
7. The Uehlfeld market along the Haupstrasse in 1899. (Courtesy of Hans Gawronski)
8. The former houses of two Rindsberg families in Uehlfeld in 1992. Rindsbergs lived in one or both of the houses at this location from the 1780s until 1938. (Courtesy of Walter Reed)
9. A page from the census of the Uehlfeld Jewish community in 1818, listing the householders, their new surnames and their children's names.
10. Problems of the Day. This lithograph and text from 1847-48 show a conversation between a Jewish peddler, who wears an Iron Cross and a lower class German friend, who sympathetically questions him about his lack of rights, as a Jew, despite being a decorated veteran. This understanding of the Jewish situation was typical of pre-1848 liberalism. (Courtesy of the Leo Baeck Institute,)
11. Photograph of an Etching of Rabbi Samson Wolf Rosenfeld. (Courtesy of the Leo Baeck Institute,)
12. A promotional postcard showing the Lutheran church, synagogue and Haupstarasse in the early 1900s. (Courtesy of Hans Gawronski)

13. Julius Rindsberg mounted during his cavalry service during the First World War.
14. The Frankfurt ghetto in 1646, engraving by Matthäus Merian, Frankfurt.
15. The Boernplatz Synagogue in Frankfurt, *c.* 1930, eight years before its destruction.
16. The first Holocaust memorial in Frankfurt, erected in 1965. The names of some Nazi-established ghettos, concentration camps and extermination centres appear around the base.
17. The Westend Synagogue in in 1992, the only one in the city to survive *Kristallnacht*.

Acknowledgements

This book relies on the facts to inform and drive the narrative. Thus, I want to first acknowledge and thank the individuals and institutions who helped me in various way obtain those facts. First, I would like to thank and acknowledge the contributions of my sister Judith Levinson, who helped find and organize many of the family documents used here and also shared with me family stories and information from my mother and father. I am grateful also and wish to thank several others who also generously shared their family history material, all of whom regrettably passed away during the years of my research: Walter Reed of Evanston, Illinois; Inge Hirsch of West Hartford, Connecticut; Johannes Gawronski of Uehlfeld, Germany; Erwin Kahn and his mother Martha Kahn of Ninevah, New York; Walter Kestler of Uehlfeld, Germany; and Hedi Karl and Gerd Beiler of Frankfurt, Germany. Others who are still with us who also shared their family histories and I also thank are Ilse Stein and her son Howie and daughter-in-law Holly of Bethesda Maryland; Margot Lax of Halendale Beach, Florida; and Helmut Haberkamm of Spardorf, Germany. Walter Reed, Erwin Kahn, Helmut Haberkamm, and Johannes Gawronski were also very generous in sharing many documents and photographs and directing me to important primary sources in . Others generously responded to my requests for specific bits of information or clarifications and I thank them for their timely help: Michael Simonson at the Leo Baeck Institute; the Stolpersteine organization in Frankfurt; Michael Lenarz at the Frankfurt Jewish Museum, John Horan, Emily Tenhundfeld, Michael Horan and Tommy Horan. I also want to acknowledge the pioneering genealogical research of the late Thea Skyte in England; Sim Seckbach and Eli Rindsberg in Florida; and Jeanne Johnson in Cincinnati all of whom generously shared their genealogies and other information, saving me and other Rindsberg, Sturm and Seckbach researchers much time and effort.

Michael Simonson also came to the rescue in arranging for the translation from German of some seventy-five letters, not a simple task because most dated to the 1939s and 1940s, were in a dozen different handwritings of varying legibility, and many were written in the Sütterlin script, used in Germany from the 1920s to 1942. Additional letters were translated by Joekie Gurski and Christiane Cunnar. Georgia Hanken of the Jewish Genealogical Society of Connecticut was most generous in sharing a copy of her manual on conducting Jewish genealogy in Germany and also lending me several books from the Society's library.

Moving from individuals to organizations, I want to thank and direct all others interested in Jewish Germany to the Leo Baeck Institute at the Center for Jewish History in New York. The institute's collection of primary and secondary materials, it expert staff, and the ever-expanding online collection, makes it the vital resource for the study of Jewish Germany. In Germany, the Stolpersteine organization in addition to its valuable work memorializing Holocaust victims also supplies another valuable service to families of victims by acquiring and supplying biographical information on those victims. The Jewish Museum in Frankfurt is the vital resource of primary and secondary sources on and also for many other Jewish communities in the region.

Although I did not know them, I want to acknowledge the research and editing contributions of Karl Schmer in Uehfeld who compiled a two-volume collection of mainly primary sources on the town's Jewish community and Johann Fleischmann who for a dozen years edited the online journal *Mesusa* which publishes articles mostly by local historians about Jewish life in Middle Franconia.

This book required considerable revision and re-working as I made decisions about what to include and exclude in order to best inform my intended audience. I had much help with this from my informal 'focus group' of Phyllis Mount, Genevieve Jackson, Meredith Swackhamer and Patricia Andreucci who patiently helped me winnow what mattered most and helped me better understand why it mattered. My partner Sharon Wirt deserves more thanks than is possible here for her continual encouragement and sometimes prodding, her sage editorial counsel, the title, and for generously giving up much shelf and closet space to my expanding research collection. Finally, I want to thank Toby Harris and Lisa Hyde at Vallentine Mitchell.

1

Engaging with Jewish Germany

This book is written for those who want a quick, wide-ranging account of the Jewish experience in Germany from the fourth century CE into the 1930s. I have written it for those curious genealogists like me, satisfied with the progress of their research, their charts filled with the names of six or seven generations of their Jewish German ancestors. But, like me, seeking more than names and dates and wanting to learn more about the Jewish experience in Germany to deepen their understanding and appreciation of their ancestor's lives.

My arrival in Jewish Germany began in June, 1992 when I accompanied my parents on a visit to Frankfurt. My mother was born in Frankfurt and became a Holocaust survivor when she fled Frankfurt to safety in London in July 1939. The 1992 trip was only my mother's second trip back, with the trip hosted by the Frankfurt government as a way of showing survivors that Germany had changed and giving them the opportunity to reconnect with their pasts. For my mother and me, it was a 'roots' trip as we drove or traveled by rail out of Frankfurt to visit four towns where her family's history had played out over several hundred years. Walking the streets of these towns, visiting the Jewish cemeteries and talking with local people spawned an endless stream of questions about what these Jewish communities had been like before they were destroyed: When did Jews first settle in there, why did they settle there, what did they do for a living, were they rich or poor, who did they marry, what form of Judaism did they practice, how did they get along with their German neighbours?

As an anthropologist long interested in community studies and especially 'outcaste' communities of forgotten peoples, I assumed that some of these questions might have been already answered by scholars or family researchers. But a dip into the literature showed that back in the early 1990s the study of now-gone German Jewish communities was best described as an emerging cottage industry. There wasn't much there and what there was focused on the nineteenth and twentieth centuries. When it came to Jews in Germany, most historians, genealogists, and the public remained consumed by the Holocaust and what interest there was on the earlier Jewish experience was a look backward, portrayals of Jewish life framed by the Holocaust and the destruction of Jewish communities across Europe.

As an anthropologist, I was drawn first to kinship, more specifically my mother's family history, beginning with compiling a full genealogy. This proved a fortuitous starting point since the trip re-kindled my mother's interest in Jewish Germany and she was more forthcoming about her past, even writing down a dozen pages of memories and producing a rough family tree. My new interest was also well timed as I soon found others beginning their journeys into Jewish genealogy. The databases and ancestry sites were not what they are now, but the family researchers were just as active and I was soon writing and talking with several other men and women in the United States, England and Germany who were working on the genealogies of three of my mother's four family lines and other related projects including gathering community records and preserving photographs and other documents. These genealogies, with their names and life dates and numbers and lines linking individuals vertically and horizontally, plus the names of spouses and places of residence, spawned all sorts of new questions about my ancestor's and the Jewish experience in Germany. But, busy with other research and writing projects, I set aside any further family research, content to have the genealogies and comforted knowing that several other individuals were at work gathering and storing the history of at least some Jewish German communities of interest to me.

Sixteen years later this desire to learn more returned and expanded beyond the genealogy research into the much larger, more ambitious project the result of which is this book. Waiting those sixteen years proved fortuitous as those years saw an enormous growth in research on Jewish communities in Germany and also much greater availability (in archives and online) of primary materials and secondary sources about Jewish German life. An accidental discovery had rekindled my interest in Germany's Jewish past. My mother had died in 2000 and my father in 2007. In the summer of 2008 my sister and I with family and friends were spending our weekends clearing out what had been my parent's summer home in the Catskill region of New York State. The bookcases, kitchen cabinets, closets, garage and chicken coop converted to a storage shed overflowed with forty years of what one friend called 'Jewish rummage sale'. One Sunday morning we took on the garage and I yanked open the bottom drawer of one of those old four-drawer file cabinets, revealing a cardboard box overflowing with letters. Quickly rifling through them we saw that many were written by our parents to each other in 1945 and 1946.

These letters were documentation of the months during the first years of their marriage when they were apart – 1945 when our mother was in London and our father on the continent as a captain with the United States Army, and 1946, when he was back home in the states and she still in

London. Stuffed in with these were many other letters, from and to several dozen other people - their mothers, aunts and uncles, cousins, employers, boyfriends, girlfriends, army buddies, and friends of friends. We counted about 500 letters. About 70 were in German, a few in Yiddish, the others all in English. Later we discovered several dozen additional letters, most of them saved by my mother in two pocketbooks she had brought from England in 1946, apparently secured there because they held special meaning for her.

The letters were only the beginning. The Catskill garage and attic yielded other family history treasures. Several boxes of my father's Second World War memorabilia including ammunition to go with several other boxes he had saved separately and of which we already knew; file folders and envelopes of documents and ephemera relevant to my mother's childhood and adolescence in Germany and England; a dresser drawer full of family photographs evidently inherited from my grandmother and a great aunt; and newspapers, magazines, playbills and all sorts ephemera an archivist would swoon over. Later in the year, we found in their Florida home more letters and documents, these neatly saved and labeled in file folders. We decided to create a 'Levinson Family Archive' and combined these new discoveries with photographs, documents, books, and ephemera we already knew about and some of which our parents had already organized into binders. The entire collection filled some twelve file boxes before I took it apart and organized it into folders, sleeves, binders, and storage envelopes.

The stash of letters had not been left in the file cabinet by accident, stuffed in the bottom drawer and forgotten over the years. My mother and father had kept them on purpose. In October 1945 my mother wrote to my father: 'Then I found myself a box to put all your letters in – what a lot there are. I guess our grandchildren will have great fun reading them. But they'd better not read mine – they would only say what a scatterbrain our grandmother must have been.' Not only did they keep the ones from 1944 and 1945 but also earlier ones, back to 1938, and my mother later added a few more letters from the 1950s, 1960s and 1970s relevant to her life in Germany and England.

The letters and other materials covered only to a slender slice of time and one family and their social circle, but they provided a starting point for what would become my much deeper and broader exploration of the Jewish experience in Germany. That exploration would take me back to the fourth century CE, into the details of Jewish life in small towns and cities, and require comparisons over time and place. I also knew that I would have to widen my enquiries beyond these communities and even Germany in general to understand the Jewish experience in the context of European and global events which had enormous influence on Jewish life in Germany including the rise of the Holy Roman Empire, the Crusades, the Enlightenment, German unification, emancipation, immigration to America and the Holocaust.

I knew that the research process would require me to wear two hats, one as my mother's son and a member of the family and descendant of the communities I was studying and a second as an anthropologist experienced, as I said, in studying forgotten or oppressed peoples including the homeless and African-American communities. The second hat would mean research and analysis at a greater emotional distance than that involved in studying my mother and her family's lives. I knew that I could not wear both hats at the same time and the exotic bits of family life that might interest me most would probably be of little interest to anyone except other family members. So, while I do include some personal family history information here, I do so mainly as way of introducing and putting a human face on more general discussions of the many aspects of Jewish life discussed throughout the book. I have tried to mostly wear my anthropologist hat and remain objective, looking for the facts, following each new fact to other facts, digging for more facts, reconciling differing accounts, questioning the trustworthiness of sources (even my mother's memory), comparing over time and place, and moving back and forth between the specific and the general.

Again, sticking to the anthropological approach, this book is mainly descriptive – who, what, where, and how – and not much about why. I am not trying to explain the big issues such as why German Jews were emancipated in the nineteenth century, or was past persecution a precursor of the Holocaust, or any other of the numerous often controversial questions about many aspects of Jewish life in Germany. When I began digging into the vast literature on Jewish Germany I quickly found that most of the thousands of books, articles, plays, poems, and films written or produced mainly in Germany, the United States, and Britain focus on the Holocaust and the Weimer Republic immediately preceding it. As with my first foray into Jewish Germany twenty years ago, books written for the general reader on the earlier periods in Jewish German history remain relatively few although certainly there are more than were available twenty years ago. More so than the general literature, what has expanded and continues to expand rapidly over the last few decades is the primary material on Jewish communities. It is not really the primary material itself that has expanded but its availability, both in print and online and also in museum and library and town and city archives. The availability of this material – censuses, administrative records, tax records, property records, church records, etc. – makes the study of the Jewish experience easier but also more difficult and time-consuming as more information brings with it more complexity, contradictions, and confusion and a greater need to provide context and make comparisons in order to produce a reasonably full and accurate account of the Jewish German experience.

As I said at the outset, the goal of this book is to provide a general description of the Jewish experience in Germany. I write with two other goals in mind. First, to provide readers with a sense of the varieties of the Jewish experience both over time and space by focusing on that experience for some 500 years in two very different communities, the small town of Uehlfeld in northern Bavaria and the major city of Frankfurt am Main and working in comparisons with other communities as well. Thus, throughout the book we move back and forth between the general and the particular, with each informing the other; the general providing context, the particular providing detail. My third goal was to provide some guidance to others contemplating research on Jewish German communities. Toward this end I provide details about my research experience here and there in the text and a broader discussion in the Methods and Sources section at the end of the book.

I have organized the book into ten chapters. The following two chapters set the stage for the subsequent chapters. In Chapter 2, I briefly set forth and discuss several of what are best labeled the *foundational patterns* of the Jewish German experience. These patterns, which include particular types of repetitive events, community structures, settlement patterns, beliefs, and political and economic processes and relationships recur over and over again across communities and over time since Jews first arrived in Germany in the early fourth century. Thus, as we look at the Jewish experience over time and places, we see how these patterns came to define and shape the German Jewish experience, even though we also find considerable variation in experience across communities and over time. In Chapter 3, I provide a chronological summary of the first 1,200 years of that experience, from the fourth century CE to the fifteenth, focusing on the emergence and persistence of these patterns. Chapters 4 and 5 then move us from the general to the specific, with a detailed description of Jewish life in Uehlfeld and other towns from about 1500 into the 1930s, with closer examination of several general topics including rural Jewish life, 'protection', Jewish-Christian relations, trading and peddling, residential patterns, and worship. In Chapter 6 I merge the discussion of several general patterns with the particulars of Jewish life in our examination of the Jewish emancipation process from the late 1700s to 1871, including the rise and spread of Reform Judaism. Chapter 7 picks up in 1871 with Jews now having full legal equality, continuing the discussion of the general and the particular as we look at the dramatic transformations in the Jewish community over the next 60 years as it transformed from an isolated, poor, rural minority into an assimilated, urban, middle class minority. In Chapters 8 and 9 we follow our Jewish ancestors from their towns to the cities, with a focus on Frankfurt am Main from about 1200 into the 1930s, looking at various features of urban life including ghetto life, international commerce, Jewish socioeconomic classes, assimilation, and the rise of the Jewish middle class. Finally, in Chapter 10 we conclude with a discussion of the Holocaust in Germany followed by a brief overview of the Jewish community in Germany today.

2
Patterns of Jewish German Life

What are we talking about here? Who were these Jews? What exactly was Germany? Just what was this German Jewish community? What do we mean by the Jewish experience? To answer these questions and many others like them, we begin with the big picture, the broad patterns that we find defining Jewish German life over time and place. These patterns fall into two broad categories. First, the demographic realities and settlement patterns of Jewish life in Germany. Second, the basic, defining and enduring social, political, economic, and religious structures, processes, and relationships, both within and outside the Jewish community.

Many people I speak to about Jewish Germany are surprised to hear that the Jewish population in German was always small. Jews were a tiny minority, almost always for all 1,800 years in Germany, rarely constituting more than 1 per cent of the overall population. From about 1400 CE on after many western European Jews had moved east, Germany's Jewish population was always much smaller than those of Poland, Lithuania, Romania and Hungry. Of course, Jews have always been a small minority wherever they have lived, excepting ancient Israel and the modern State of Israel. Today, Jews constitute about .15 per cent of Germany's population, compared to 1.8 per cent in the United States, .74 per cent in France, .5 per cent in the United Kingdom. It makes some sense that people would get the impression that there were a lot of Jews in Germany, given the Nazi obsession with Jews and the Holocaust. But, even in 1933 when Hitler came to power, Jews in Germany numbered only about 525,000, about .8 per cent of the population. And the continuing attention given the Holocaust over the last 50 years, although most victims were not German Jews, might well also lead to people to assume that German Jewry was quite large. Another possible cause of this misperception is Jews in the United States who are descendants of German Jews, most of whom fled to the United States in the mid-1800s, are far fewer in number than the descendants of Eastern European Jews, who arrived later in the century and in the early twentieth century.

That they have always been numerically few, should not mask the fact that Jews have lived in Germany for a long time, for over seventeen centuries, dating back to the arrival of the first migrants who moved north from Italy in the early fourth century, or perhaps even earlier. Despite hundreds of expulsions and massacres over the centuries, some Jewish communities have always existed somewhere in Germany. This distinguishes the Jewish experience in Germany from many other European nations such as Poland and Lithuania whose Jewish populations arrived much later and also from nations such as England, France, Spain, and Portugal which at times had Jewish communities and at other times had none, having expelled all their Jewish residents and/or forcing some to convert to Christianity.

But, there is an important qualifier to the continual presence of Jewish communities in Germany. While we find Jewish communities always existing somewhere in Germany, Jews never lived everywhere in Germany. Rather, Jewish communities were unevenly dispersed across the German territories before 1871 and across the unified nation after then. The breadth and unevenness of this dispersal becomes clear if we visualize a map with red pins marking the location of every Jewish community that ever existed in Germany. We'd be looking at a map dotted with several thousand pins, but some regions would have hundreds of pins while others would have none or just a few. And when look more closely at those regions like Franconia in Bavaria where there are lots of pins, we would see that they too are unevenly distributed, with clusters here and there amid open spaces. Most generally, the map shows us that Jewish communities were concentrated in the west; eastern Germany always had very few Jewish communities and so too did much of Bavaria. And even in the west we find considerable variation: some towns and cities had Jewish communities while many towns never had a Jewish community. What the pins can't show us, because they don't factor in the time dimension, is that many towns and cities sometimes had and sometimes didn't have a Jewish community. In many towns and cities Jewish communities were expelled or driven off by massacres and attempts at forced conversion to Christianity and at some later date sometimes just a few years other times a few centuries, Jews were readmitted and they established a new Jewish community. In some communities, this pattern of expulsion followed by re-admittance repeated itself several times, especially in the sixteenth and seventeenth centuries.

Putting aside the map and broadening our analysis from the distribution of Jewish communities to the distribution of Jewish families and individuals, the landscape of Jewish communities gets even more complicated. Jewish communities varied in size, with some at times quite large, with populations far exceeding the less than 1 per cent average across Germany. Most Jewish communities, including neighboring ones of larger communities, were always small and some communities had only visiting Jews, mainly traveling Jewish traders and peddlers. Thus, in regions with larger Jewish population, most Jews lived in only a few towns and cities. Typically these were cities (though not all cities and sometimes not even nearby ones) or market towns, which attracted Jewish traders. Two such towns were Uehlfeld and Burghaslach, discussed in Chapters 4 through 7; each had Jewish communities that constituted at least 25 per cent of the town's population at times in the 1700s and 40 per cent in the 1800s.

The uneven distribution of Jewish communities across Germany mirrored or perhaps in some ways was even responsible for the uneven experience of Jewish communities in Germany, across both time and place. We can see this variation in both distribution and experience by comparing the Jewish experiences for the three centuries (about 1500 into the 1800s) in two cities significant in Jewish history, Nuremberg and Fürth. The cities are located just six miles apart in Franconia, now part of Bavaria, but before 1800 a distinct region. Given their proximity, we might expect that the two Jewish communities would have similar experiences. In fact, they couldn't have been more different during these three hundred years. Nuremberg, then and now, was the larger city, known today in Jewish history and world history for its role as the propaganda headquarters for the National Socialist German Workers' Party (Nazi Party or NSDAP) in the 1920s and 1930s, the Nuremberg laws of 1935, and as the setting for the post-World War II tribunals. But despite its role in recent Jewish German history, during these three earlier centuries, Nuremberg had no Jewish history as it was one of a number of cities with no Jewish community. The city's officials expelled the entire community in 1499. The immediate rationale for the expulsion was a church ruling forbidding Jews from collecting interest on loans to Christians, although it followed several decades of increasing restrictions on Jewish economic activity. The decision pleased German farmers and craftsmen, many of whom owned Jewish moneylenders what they had borrowed plus interest, but deprived the Jewish community of its major source of income and it was expelled when it objected to the law. Nuremberg officials saw the expulsion as permanent, and bought up Jewish property and even destroyed the Jewish cemetery, repurposing some stones for use in buildings and walls. But, as was often the case, the exile did not last forever, although it was not until the 1840s that Jews were permitted to begin re-establishing their community, when during the emancipation era Jews moved to Nuremberg from nearby small towns and helped establish Nuremberg as a thriving commercial and transportation centre.

Fürth is labelled Nuremberg's twin city, but for Jews over those same three centuries the cities were nothing more than fraternal twins. There was nothing identical, nothing even similar, about the Jewish experience in the two cities. Jews first settled in Fürth in the early fifteenth century but were expelled in 1478. They returned in 1528 and created a vibrant Jewish community, at times in the 1600s the largest and most influential in Germany. The community's growth and influence was aided by the arrival of immigrants from Vienna and Russia, both groups fleeing persecution and bringing with them political and economic experiences new to rural Germany. Among the community's achievements were the first Jewish hospital in Germany in 1653, a yeshiva in 1657, Jewish printing houses in 1691 and an orphanage in 1697. The yeshiva became the center of rabbinical scholarship and teaching, luring eager thirteen-year-old scholars to its six-year rabbinical curriculum in the 'The Franconian Jerusalem'. The Fürth community not only survived but thrived because of the political acumen of its leaders, who astutely played off against one another the competing desires of the Protestant Church in Bamberg, the rulers of Nuremburg, and margrave of the neighboring territory of Ansbach, whom waged a 300-year competition for control of Fürth. Jewish influence was so great that in 1652 they were awarded two seats on the city council and in 1719 the unprecedented right of self -government, including a Jewish court to settle disputes in the Jewish community.

1. Artistic Rendering of the New Shul and Old Shul; Fuerth, c. 1705. (Courtesy of the Leo Baeck Institute, New York)

The contrasting experiences in Nuremberg and Fürth tell the story; there has never been a single experience defining all of the Jewish communities in Germany over the seventeen centuries in which Jews have lived there. There was a common Jewish identity and almost always everywhere a status as outsiders in a Christian society and community life defined by the central patterns of the Jewish experience we are discussing here, but still there was a variety of experience that varied often widely over place and time. Even in the Nazi Era (c.1920-1945) the experiences were different, although in the end they were much the same – exile or death for individuals – social and physical destruction of the communities. And after the spread of Reform Judaism in the nineteenth century, there was no single faith community either. Thus, the Jewish experience is best approached anthropologically, from the ground up, by focusing on the experience of particular communities or clusters of communities within the context of these broad patterns which themselves both shaped and were shaped by the local and regional experiences. This means, as again suggested above, moving back and forth from the particular to the general, back and forth from description to comparison.

   The Jewish German experience varied because the communities were small, dispersed, and concentrated and also because the German territories themselves did not share a single experience, as the British historian Neil McGregor reminds us:

> [It is] impossible to write a general history of Germany like that of France or England because for so long what is now Germany was many politically separate units. The Holy Roman Empire provided some sense of common identity and structure but hardly ruled the numerous units which differed and at times were in conflict with one another. (McGregor, 2015).

McGregor's point needs to be stressed and remembered – when we describe the Jewish experience in Germany, we are really describing the experiences of particular Jewish communities or clusters of communities which existed within the many (sometimes over three hundred) Germanic states, principalities, duchies, margraviates, church-owned lands, and free imperial cities which today make up the nation of Germany. This array of political units of varying sizes, shapes, wealth, and power emerged in the early middle ages and existed into the nineteenth century. They consolidated over the nineteenth century as the remaining Germans states unified to form the German nation in 1871. Although for a thousand years under the nominal rule of the Holy Roman Empire, these separate polities were each ruled by its own prince, duke, count, margrave, bishop, or city council, with each ruler harboring his own territorial and economic ambitions and aided by his own court, ministers and administrators, laws and regulations, army, and currency. It was these powerful men, aided by their ministers and administrators, who decided whether or not Jews could live in their territory, in which particular towns or cities they could live, and for how long they could continue to live there. Jews who were permitted to live in their towns or cities were 'protected' by the ruler, a distinct legal status which along with the Jewish community's devotion to Judaism (its laws, rituals, and institutions) and their earning their livings by way of 'Jewish' occupations marked them as fundamentally different from and kept them apart from their Christian German neighbours and customers. Separation based on religion was a two-way street with German Christian hostility toward Jews and Judaism dating to the fourth century just as strong a segregating force as was Jewish adherence to Judaism. It was this religion-based hostility that often led to anti-Jewish stereotyping, demonizing, scapegoating, assaults, massacres, attempts at forced conversions and expulsions.

Returning to 'protection', it was an odd form of protection, as what was really protected was the economic interests of the ruler, the religious anti-Semitism of the church, and the jealousy and resentment of the German peasants and craftsmen. Protection in the form of laws and regulations governing Jewish life and protection letters (one-sided contracts) with Jewish men and sometimes women typically limited the number of Jewish families in a town or city, restricted their economic activities to trading and peddling, kept most of them poor, levied heavy taxes and fees, and sometimes regulated their practice of Judaism. Although individual Jewish families might have some choice in where they lived among communities which allowed 'protected' Jews, it was mainly a ruler's self-interest and territorial, political, and economic competition between rulers which determined whether or not a Jewish community was allowed to form and remain in region or in a particular town or city. The ruler's self-interest was about wealth as Jewish communities provided revenues for the ruler through the high taxes they paid and the income they generated from trading mainly farm products such as grain, hops, and cattle produced by the German peasants.

Thus, Jewish communities were established and allowed to remain when the ruler saw them as an economic asset. Some rulers also saw them as a political asset when competing with other rulers for wealth and territory, and those rulers would welcome Jewish families from rival territories, sometimes enticing them away from rivals, and more often welcoming them when they were expelled by rulers who no longer found them economically useful. It was this dynamic of expulsions from one community followed by protection in another that ensured that Jews usually had somewhere to settle in Germany from the eighth century on. Local and regional church officials (Catholic and later Lutheran as well) also played a key role in the fate of Jewish communities. Bishops, priests and pastors were often, though not always, more opposed than the ruler to the presence or expansion of a Jewish community in their town or city and viewed expulsion as the appropriate remedy, a desire that often put them at odds with the ruler who wanted Jewish taxes and trading acumen. Thus, Jewish communities often found themselves caught (which astute Jewish leaders could sometimes play to their benefit) between the competing economic and religious agendas of the secular rulers and the church officials.

2. An eighteenth century etching labelled 'Jude' showing a poor Jewish peddler or beggar. (Courtesy of the Leo Baeck Institute, New York)

Finally, as regards Jewish settlement in Germany, we also need to remember that the German states did not operate in a vacuum; quite to the contrary, events in other nations always affected Jewish settlement and life in Germany. Jews were not indigenous to Germany, with the first settlers moving there from Italy and France. Following several centuries of relative freedom, the twelfth into the fifteenth centuries, proved especially harsh (massacres, forced conversions, mass suicides, expulsions) and many German Jews fled east to Poland where they were accepted by local rulers who valued their trading and business skills. Several centuries later, when persecutions increased in Poland, some returned to Germany. And then, in the nineteenth century, German Jews were a small but significant part of the massive immigration from Germany to America and in the twentieth from Germany to America, Israel, England, South America and elsewhere.

Although it is hardly the whole story, the Jewish experience in Germany for most of its seventeen centuries has often been a struggle for survival. Jewish communities often did not enjoy nor could count on future stability. Entire communities were at times massacred, fled, or expelled and never reconstituted or, as we saw in Nuremberg, reconstituted only many years or centuries later. Individual communities grew and contracted as individuals and families sought better opportunities by either moving in or moving out. Jewish communities began experiencing greater stability in the late seventeenth and early eighteenth centuries following the re-population of Germany (and much of Europe) as the continent recovered from the devastating Thirty Years' War. The quest for civil, economic, religious, and political rights began in the latter half of the eighteenth century, with Germany's Jews finally fully emancipated across all of Germany in 1871 when the German states unified into a single nation. But even then the Jewish experience continued to vary, as regional economics, the political interests of the German states, rural-urban variations, and old regional patterns of discrimination never fully disappeared despite the legal grant of equality.

This portrayal of Jewish life in Germany as a continual struggle for survival must be balanced by the recognition that not all of Jewish life in the German states was harsh, unstable, confining or exacting. But, the truth is that we know far less about the inner life of Jewish communities than we do about their public life which mostly involved economic and political relationships (or the absence thereof) with Christian Germans. We know far less because we have less of a record of these Jewish communities written by the communities themselves. As part of the persecution of Jews, much of that early record was destroyed. But, even the records kept by German officials for their own administrative and financial purposes let us see that Jewish communities were often vibrant communities, the residents unified by bonds of kinship, marriage, economic cooperation, and their faith. Parents arranged their children's marriages and sang and danced at their weddings, cried at the many funerals for their infants and children, walked or rode in carts or wagons to visit kin in nearby and distant towns and cities, baked bread in communal ovens, brawled in the street and debated the Talmud late into the night. Communities selected leaders, managed relations between their few rich and many poor, built their synagogues, hired school teachers, maintained their cemeteries, and enforced Jewish law. One has the clear impression that Jewish men and women and their children lived in two world – the often uncertain, restricted, and harsh world of Christian Germany and the private, rich, nourishing world of their communities, a dual existence common to all outcaste peoples such as African-Americans, the homeless and the Dalits (formerly labelled untouchables) in India.

Jewish families were large (although the infant mortality rate was high as elsewhere in Europe) into the nineteenth century, and despite the coming and going of families and entire communities, especially from about 1700 on, some families lived in their towns and cities for generations, becoming the core and bearers of the histories of their communities, as other individuals and families came and went. Jewish men and women worked hard, developed valuable business skills and networks, and many placed great importance on educating their children, first in Judaism and later in general education as well. Jewish communities as soon as they were settled and had a large enough population and sufficient funds, built their community institutions – synagogue, cemetery, *mikvah*, and school and retained the religious specialists – a rabbi in only a few communities, a cantor, *shochet*, teacher, and kosher butcher in most. When Jews were afforded freedom and opportunity in the nineteenth century, their community spirit, hard work, business experience, and valuing of education paid off and many prospered, rapidly becoming an assimilated, urban, middle and upper-middle class segment of German society. Yet, anti-Jewish sentiments and actions, while muted at times, never ended and freedom and opportunity contracted rapidly with the rise of Nazism in the 1920s and then disappeared after the Nazis came to power in 1933.

With these central demographic, settlement, economic, political, and religious patterns in mind we can move on in the following chapter to a quick historical survey of the Jewish experience in Germany from first arrival in the early fourth century CE into the sixteenth century. It was over these centuries that these patterns of Jewish life emerged and took hold and also it was over these centuries that the Jewish experience diversified. This is a long stretch of time and regrettably we know far less about the Jewish experience for much of it than we would like. Nonetheless, the Jewish experience is well-worth outlining in the context of the major events of the Dark Ages, Middle Ages and Early Modern Period during which many of the overarching patterns of Jewish experience first appeared and then defined Jewish life in its various forms over the centuries.

3

A Quick Historical Tour

Historians know all too well that the further back we go in time, the less we are likely to know. Archaeology can fill in some gaps such as the recent excavation of a synagogue dating to about 800 CE in Mainz, but the archaeology of Jewish Germany is in its infancy. *Not knowing very much about is especially true for peoples like German Jews who were few in number and whose early history was mostly recorded in the official records kept by those in power, rendering them in the words of anthropologist Eric Wolf, a 'people without history'.* Thus, what we know of Jewish life in Germany for its first seven hundred years or so is incomplete and open to speculation and interpretation. Our ability to understand Jewish life in those centuries and even in later ones can also be hindered by the tendency to interpret the Jewish past in Germany through the lens of the Holocaust, the best-described and most-interpreted period in Jewish history. For example, it is impossible to ignore the centuries of persecutions (massacres, forced conversions, expulsions) and then easy to interpret them as antecedents of or part of an ongoing pattern that ultimately produced the Holocaust. There are certainly linkages between earlier and later events (one being that in communities where persecution of Jews was harsh in the past it was also harsh in the Holocaust period), but viewing the past from the sensibilities of the present comes with the cost of drawing our attention away from other aspects of the past Jewish experience which may have varied from place to place, or changed in meaningful ways over time.

Although our knowledge of this lengthy time period is limited, we certainly have enough information to see the emergence of several of the patterns of Jewish life outlined in the previous chapter. These include the dispersed/concentrated settlement pattern; devotion to Judaism with alterations in practice to conform to a Christian world; rabbis and scholars as community leaders and agents of change; involvement in trade and moneylending; 'protection' by local and regional rulers with restrictions on civil and political rights; conflict between secular and clerical officials over Jewish rights; social and residential segregation and church-inspired persecution.

Beginning our exploration of the Jewish German experience with what we know with reasonable confidence, it seems likely that Jews were living in settlements near the Rhine River in west-central Germany by the early fourth century CE. Evidence of a Jewish presence comes from two orders issued by the Roman Emperor Constantine in 321 and 331 CE concerning the Jewish community in Cologne. Cologne was a Roman colony and perhaps the locale of the first Jewish community in Germany. Other early settlements may have been in Worms, Treves, and Mainz. The 321 order removed the exemption given Jews in the colony from serving on the *curia*, the city council. The second one, ten years later, exempted both Christian church officials and Jewish synagogue officials from service on the *curia*. That Jews were now expected to serve on the *curia* tells us that Jews lived in Cologne and also suggests that some Jews were wealthy, as the *curia's* main function was to collect tribute for the emperor, which *curia* members had to pay themselves if not enough was raised from the colony's farmers and artisans. For this reason, some wealthy non-Jewish men shunned service, creating the need to recruit members from the Jewish community. Presumably, these Jewish men were also wealthy, although how they gained that wealth is not known but it may have been from winemaking and trading.

We also are fairly certain that these first Jewish settlers came to Germany from southern Italy. And, again we are fairly certain that these first settlers were themselves Jewish, descendants of Jews who had settled in southern Europe beginning about 150 BCE, migrating there from southwest Asia, primarily from the eastern Mediterranean region that now includes the nations of Lebanon, Syria, and Israel. These Jewish immigrants to southern Europe farmed and traded and they actively sought converts to Judaism among their southern European neighbours. Many who converted were European women who married and had children with Jewish men, the children being raised Jewish. A trickle of Jews kept crossing the Mediterranean in the following years until 70 CE when a large influx arrived following the destruction of the Jerusalem Temple. But these later settlers did not seek converts nor intermarry with non-Jews, the Romans having banned conversion to Judaism in 1 CE.

The descendants of these first Jewish settlers in southern Europe moved north near the Rhine with other migrants from Italy. Once there, they maintained their Jewish identity and probably lived and farmed among non-Christian Germanic peoples already settled in the region. Emperor Constantine had declared Christianity the religion of the Roman Empire in 312 CE, but it not take hold in northern Europe into the end of the century. Conventional wisdom has long held that these Jewish settlers in Germany were the descendants of Jewish men and Jewish women who traced their ancestry to Jews in southwest Asia. Recent DNA analysis of modern Eastern European Jews (Ashkenazim) tells us that the ethnic ancestry of these first settlers was actually more complex. They were, as long believed, descended from Jewish men and women, but only on the male side were they descended from Jewish men originally from southwest Asia. On the female side, their ethnic ancestry was different. They were mostly descended from the European women in southern European who had converted to Judaism and married Jewish men. And after Jewish communities were established in Germany this pattern of converting and marrying European women resumed on a limited scale, leaving the genomes of the descendants of these early settlers even more 'European'.

This DNA-based finding has implications for European Jewish ancestry beyond the ancestry of these first settlers and their immediate descendants. The DNA researchers report: '80% of Ashkenazi maternal ancestry is due to the assimilation of MtDNAs indigenous to Europe...' (Costa et al., 2013). They are referring to Ashkenazi Jews in the world today, that is, Jews of Central and Eastern European ancestry who constitute the majority (about eighty percent) of Jews around the world. 'Ashkenaz' is the Hebrew word first used to label Jews who lived in northern France and Western Germany in the Middle Ages and has remained in use as the generic name for Jews in Eastern Europe (Poland, Russia, Lithuania) who were descended in large part from German Jews who migrated east beginning in the twelfth century. Because Ashkenazim today are descended to a significant extent from German Jews, they too, as the DNA analysis shows, are of mixed ancestry – Jewish men from southwest Asia and Jewish women from southern Europe. Thus, these first Jewish settlers along the Rhine were an especially significant population in Jewish history, as a major ancestral population of most Jews alive today. Beyond ancestry and genealogy, this finding has important political implications as it supports the Zionist claim that Israel is the Jewish homeland. The DNA evidence also questions the alternative fringe theory that Ashkenazim are descended from the Khazars, a group in the Caucasus, whose leaders and elite allegedly converted to Judaism in the eight century CE. Of course, DNA research continues and based on previous twists and turns we can anticipate refinement of the general pattern outlined above.

We know very little about these first settlers, not even where they lived, other than Cologne, nor about Jewish life in Germany in the following several hundred years. It is assumed that Jews were few in number and confined mainly to settlements near the Rhine where they farmed and traded and until Christianity took root, lived in ways much like their non-Jewish neighbors. As the Roman Empire's power declined in the fifth century

Europe fell into the Dark Ages, some three hundred years of poverty, violence, and dislocations as the Ostrogoths, Visigoths, Vandals, Huns, Franks, Burgundians, both converts to Christianity and pagan, battled for control. Jews probably suffered along with other peoples and at times were singled out for harsh treatment as the Church promulgated beliefs labeling Jews as enemies of Christianity and enacted laws restricting Jewish civil and political rights including prohibiting Jews from holding positions in government, marrying Christians, testifying against Christians, owning slaves and seeking converts to Judaism. But some Jewish communities prospered and grew under benevolent rulers and church leaders including Pope Gregory (c. 540 – 604) who banned the forced conversion of Jews and Theodoric the Great of Italy (454 -526) who encouraged Jewish settlement leading to the establishment of Jewish communities by 500 CE in Avignon and Marseille, France and in Genoa, Livorno, Ravenna, Venice, and Pola, Italy. Some in these communities were traders and money lenders and we see here the emergence of a Jewish commercial class who would come to play a leading economic role as international traders moving goods and money across and in and out of Europe and as financiers for the nobility and the church.

The fight for control of Central Europe concluded with the decline of the Roman Empire in the fifth century and Franks in control of France and western Germany. The Frankish Kingdom expanded under Charlemagne (r. 768-814) who, seeking to expand his kingdom and recognizing the wider regional and international market for the kingdom's agricultural products, encouraged Jews and especially experienced traders to move north from cities in northern Italy and southern France. Seizing this new opportunity, Jews again migrated north through the Alps and up the Rhone Valley beginning in about 500 CE and by 1000 CE Jewish communities were established and some flourishing in Augsburg, Ratisbon, Prague, Wurzberg, Mainz, Worms, Speyer, Metz, Verdun, Cologne, Merseburg and Magdeburg, all on or near major riverine trade routes along the Rhine, Main, Danube, Meuse, and Moselle.

Traders were given special privileges and protection to encourage their freedom to travel and compete with Christian traders but Jews had to pay higher taxes and their civil and political rights continued to be restricted. Restrictions and special conditions included: Jews being required to produce four, seven, or nine witnesses when to bringing charges against a Christian whom needed only three against a Jew; a ban on employing Christians on Sunday; an exemption for church property as collateral on loans; segregation in Jewish neighborhoods or streets; and Jews being required to take a unique and demeaning 'Jew Oath' in legal situations requiring oath taking, a common judicial truth-seeking method in the Middle Ages.

With the support of the rulers and a steady supply of products from peasant farmers and craftsmen, Jews in Germany, France, and Italy took control of substantial segments of the local, regional, and international trade. But Jewish traders did not monopolize any segment of the markets, as Christians traded as well and were supported by trade guilds which excluded Jews. In Germany, Jewish traders operating in the local or regional markets traded clothing, wine, farm produce, and salt. They often found themselves in competition with the Christian traders who complained about unfair Jewish business practices and were sometimes successful in convincing local authorities to limit Jewish trade. But Jewish traders were usually tolerated because their involvement in wide trade networks provided them with a wider range of products, they offered lower prices, they extended credit, and their wider product line appealed to both the wealthy and the peasants. Jewish involvement in trade combined with their status as an outcaste religious and social group, produced what became the typical two-track interaction pattern between Jews and Christian Germans, in which Jewish and Christian individuals (and by extension, the Jewish and German communities) out of necessity maintained regular economic relationships, but interacted little with one another in other spheres of life, worshipped separately, and often lived apart.

Internationally, Jewish traders who would travel the roads and seas for months or years at a time, operated across Europe, into North Africa and as far east as China. They bought and sold oils, amber, textiles, hides, armaments, spices, precious stones and slaves from and to their wealthy and powerful clients including royal and noble courts and both the secular and clerical (Christian and Muslim) aristocracies. As with local and regional trading, they had several advantages over their Christian rivals including international experience, trading networks of relatives or other Jewish traders, fluency in several trade languages, and financial and mathematical skills that enabled them to deal in and convert different currencies. Perhaps, most importantly they were politically neutral, neither Christian nor Muslim nor citizens of nations dominated by the two religions. This allowed them to cross national borders (for a fee) in Europe closed to Muslims and those in Asia and Africa closed to Christians. But, competition with Christians took its toll and at times made trading more difficult or less lucrative. Business suffered in the late 900s when the Venetians and other Italian trading cities banned Jews from their vessels, limiting Jewish travel across the Mediterranean to Africa and the East. Jewish opportunities declined further east in that same century as markets closed due to political unrest in China and Central Asia. And later, as the Hansa commercial cities became dominant in northern Europe, international trading opportunities shrunk there as well.

The best known (to us) and most successful of the European Jewish traders were a group known as the Radhanites who operated between about 500 and 1000 CE, moving into a trade vacuum created by the decline of the Roman Empire. It is not clear just who these people were, possibly a loose network of Jewish traders, a kinship network such as a clan, or really just Jewish international traders in general. The following description of their activities and routes by the Muslim official ibn Kohrdadbeh in the ninth century shows just how extensive their activities were and the vital commercial role they played in the emerging global economy.

> These merchants speak Arabic, Persian, Roman (i.e. Greek and Latin), the Frank, Spanish, and Slavic languages. They journey from west to east, from east to west, partly on land, partly by sea. They transport from the west eunuchs, female slaves, boys, brocade, castor, marten, and other furs, and swords. They take ship Firanja (France), on the Western Sea, and make for Farama (Pelusium). There they load their goods on camel-backs, and go by land to al-Kolzum (Suez), a distance of twenty-five farsakhs (parasangs). They embark in the East Sea (Red Sea) and sail from al-Kolzum to al-Jar (port of Medina) and Jeddah (port of Mecca), then they go to Sind, India, and China. On their return from China they carry back musk, aloes, camphor, cinnamon, and other products of the Eastern countries to al-Kolzum, and bring them to Farama, where they again embark on the Western Sea. Some make sail for Constantinople to sell their goods to the Romans; others go to the palace of the king of the Franks to place their goods.
>
> Sometimes these Jew merchants, when embarking in the land of the Franks in the Western Sea, making for Antioch (at the mouth of the Orontes); thence by land to Al-Jabia (? Al-Hanaya on the bank of the Euphrates), where they arrive after three days' march. There they embark on the Euphrates and reach Baghdad, whence they sail down the Tigris to al-Obolla. From al-Obolla they sail for Oman, Sind, Hind, and China. All this is connected one with another.
>
> These different journeys can also be made by land. The merchants who start from Spain or France go to Sus al-Akza (Morocco), and then to Tangier, whence they walk to Africa (Kairouan) (Tunisia), and the capital of Egypt. Thence they go to ar-Ramla, visit Damascus, Al-Kufa, Baghdad, and al-Basra (Bassora), cross Ahwaz, Fars, Kirman, Sind, Hind, and arrive at China. Sometimes, also, they take the route behind

Rome, and passing through the country of the Slavs, arrive at Khamlij, the capital of the Khozars. They embark on the Jorjan Sea, arrive at Balkh, betake themselves from there across the Oxus and continue their journey toward the Yurt, Toghozghor, and from there to China.
(Source: ibn Khordadbeh, *The Book of Ways and Kingdoms*. C. 817, in Adler, pp. 2-3)

Returning to the political situation in Germany, in the ninth century Jews found themselves subjects of the Holy Roman Empire, established when Pope Leo III crowned Charlemagne emperor, the first one to hold the title in three hundred years. At times, the Holy Roman Empire encompassed territory within the boundaries of modern-day Germany, Austria, Belgium, Luxembourg, the Czech Republic, Switzerland, France and Poland. Germany formed the largest territory and portions of it remained in the Empire until 1815, although the Empire's authority had diminished long before then. In fact, the Holy Roman Empire was never a strong, centralized state as were France and England in the ninth century. Rather, from the beginning it was a church-sponsored geopolitical entity that provided an overarching political, legal, and religious structure that by the late ninth century had decentralized into what at times would be over three hundred smaller political units each ruled by a prince, duke, or noble of lesser rank or a church official such as bishop. A few cities were 'imperial free cities', ruled directly by the emperor while other cities were ruled by the regional ruler and city council. Jewish communities, of course, were ruled by the prince or duke or bishop in whose polity they were permitted to live, a political arrangement that would characterize Jewish community life into the nineteenth century.

The period from the late tenth century into the twelfth century is labeled by some the 'Golden Age' of German Jewry. This is somewhat of an overstatement and like much about Jewish German life, pertains to some segments of the population but not to everyone. It was a golden age for wealthy traders in some cities and the rabbis and scholars supported by their wealth who reinterpreted Jewish practice to fit the Central European cultural environment. But many Jews, whose lives we know much less about, remained poor and subsisted by trading locally and loaning money to a distrusting Christian population. The Golden Age was centered in the *Shum* (*Schum, ShUM*) cities/communities of Mainz, Speyer and Worms. The name, Shum, is an acronym formed from the first letters of the Hebrew names for these three cities. The name signifies the interaction among rabbis and scholars across these communities resulting in the formation of a confederation of Jewish communities in the thirteenth century. As with much in the German Jewish experience, the Golden Age was enabled by supportive rulers, in this case bishops, who protected Jewish communities and employed traders who, in turn, became wealthy and supported rabbis and scholars and Jewish institutions in these cities. Among the dozens of leading rabbis and scholars whose ideas and innovations in Jewish thought and practice remained influential for many centuries were Gershom Me'or Hagola (c. 960 – 1040) ('The Light of the Exile'), Torah and Talmud commentator Rashi (1040 – 1105), Talmudist Meir ben Baruch (1215- 1293), and the student of Jewish life Yaakov haLevi (1375 – 1293). Certainly the first two remain familiar to Hebrew school students today.

The collective study, documentation, and interpretation by these and other rabbis and scholars redefined Jewish cultural traditions and religious practices previously established in Babylon, Jerusalem, the eastern Mediterranean, and northern France (where the Golden Age really began in Troyes) to fit to social, political and economic contexts of Jewish life in Christian Germany and France. Their new prescriptions for Jewish daily life and religious practice would become the norm for Ashkenazi communities in Germany and France and later in Jewish diaspora communities in Eastern

3. Gravestones in an older section of the Worms Jewish Cemetery, thought to be the oldest surviving one in Europe.

Europe with some continuing to serve as accepted Jewish practice in the twenty-first century. The prescriptions cut across all aspects of Jewish life: Romanesque architecture in synagogues, distinctive synagogues for women allowing greater female involvement in the worship service, monumental ritual baths, a ban on plural marriage, private correspondence with rabbis, documentation of Jewish customs, real life events as the basis for legal decisions, new liturgical compositions, mourning prayers and the early Hasidic movement of the twelfth and thirteen centuries. Thus, the Shum communities became the major center of Jewish learning and teaching in Central Europe and today their history and physical remains (cemeteries, excavated synagogues, *mikvahs,* and other structures) serve as important reminders of and memorials to the shaping role of Jewish Germany in the subsequent Jewish diaspora.

The combination of massacres, expulsions, and mass suicides in the Jewish communities in western Germany as the Crusaders rampaged south during the first Crusade in 1096 is often cited as the event and year that brought the so-called 'Golden Age' to an abrupt and unexpected end. In fact several of these Jewish communities with the support of local bishops did reconstitute themselves after the attacks and Jewish scholarship continued, though on a more limited scale, for several more centuries. But, it is certainly true that the Crusades (eight from 1095 to 1270-72) along with the decline of feudalism, more economic opportunities for Christians beyond farming and the crafts and increased church-led persecution of Jews and rejection of Judaism, dramatically altered life in Jewish communities in Christian Europe. In addition, the Crusades and the religious fervor behind it led to a basic reorientation of the place of Jews in Europe. Jews had always or nearly always been outsiders, but they were outsiders as we have seen with a clear and necessary economic role that benefitted those in power. The Crusader worldview, driven by the goal of freeing the Holy Land from Muslim rule as part of the broader war between Christianity and Islam, classified all non-Christians including Jews, heretics, and those inclined to a more rational, scientific view of the world, as enemy peoples who were to be dealt with by either integration into Christian society by converting to Christianity or dropping their heretical beliefs, or by being removed by being driven out or killed off or forced to live apart in segregated neighbourhoods or streets.

The Crusades posed a real physical danger to Jewish communities while the other economic and social changes across Europe mentioned above, posed an economic danger by reducing the market for Jewish traders who had played a leading role in the international and regional trade. Jewish traders now had much competition from Christian traders who took advantage of new trade routes to the east and south opened by the Crusaders. By the time these new Christian traders enter the marketplace, Jewish trade was already declining, with some Mediterranean ports closed to them. The Crusades and their aftermath inflicted further damage. The new trade routes and even long-established ones were no longer safe or fertile for Jewish traders who were now denied entrance to towns and cities and markets and regularly verbally and physically assaulted during their travels.

As Jewish trade declined, Jews more than ever turned to money lending as their primary means of support. In the past money lending often in the form of extending credit had been integrated with trading, but now money lending stood alone and was increasingly seen as a Jewish occupation, with Jewish money lenders depicted as dishonest, unscrupulous, and much too eager to take advantage of illiterate peasants. Although the church banned usury, some Christians did lend money as well, although they were relatively few, leaving money lending as a mainly Jewish activity. The Jewish money lender become the stereotype of the European Jew, rendered in drawing, painting, and sculpture as an old, bearded man seated behind a wooden table handing money to the Christian peasant standing humbled before him.

The extreme persecutions of Jewish communities during the First Crusade marked the beginning of four centuries of atrocities against the Jewish communities across Central and Western Europe. The list of atrocities is far too wide and long to provide here, but a highlight reel of the worst and those with long-term ramifications would surely include the following.

1096	Massacres, forced conversions, suicides, extortion of protection money by Crusaders (mainly lesser nobles and peasants) in Speyer, Worms, Mainz, Cologne, Regensberg, Metz and Prague and other cities. Church officials and some citizens protected Jews, other collaborated with the Crusaders, and most remained indifferent.
1100s	The first Jewish ghettos are stablished in Portugal and Spain.
1144	The first recorded 'blood libel' in Norwich, England. Jews are charged with the ritual murder of Christian children to obtain their blood to use in preparing *matzah* for Passover. The blood libel spread across Europe and continues in some Eastern European nations in the twenty-first century.
1215	At the Fourth Lateran Council, called by Pope Innocent III, a decree is enacted requiring Jews to wear special dress, badges or distinctive conical hats, to distinguish them from other people. The decree is not uniformly enforced.

1243	Jews in Belitz, Germany are charged with desecrating the host, the sacred wafer or bread distributed to worshippers during Eucharist, an especially serious crime against Jesus and Christianity. Jews were charged with damaging the host causing it to bleed, which was actually red or orange mold that appears naturally on stale bread. The accused Jews in Belitz and in following centuries especially in Germany, France, and Poland are killed, often by burning.
1290	Jews are expelled from England.
1306, 1394	Jews are expelled from France.
1348-1350	During the Plague or Black Death, which killed about one-third of the European population, Jews in many locales are blamed for the plague, often accused of purposefully poisoning wells. Jews so accused are expelled and massacred. The fourteenth century was a difficult one in Europe with poor harvest, famine in addition to the plague and severe depopulation. Jews become the scapegoats for all these disasters.
1442-43	Jews are expelled from the Netherlands.
1463	A ghetto is established in Frankfurt am Main.
1492	Jews are forced to convert or expelled from Spain.
1496-98	Jews are expelled from Portugal.
1516	A ghetto is established in Venice, Italy, leading to the use of the label, ghetto, for segregated, walled, and locked Jewish neighbourhoods in European cities.

In addition to these major persecutions, the period from the late 1300s into the 1500s were two and one-half centuries of frequent and regular expulsions from German cities and towns including from Cologne, Mainz, Augsburg, Breslau, Wurzberg, Nuremberg, Bayreuth, Hamburg and Brandenburg as well as all of the states of Saxony, Bavaria, and Austria. As we discuss in later chapters, Jewish communities were later reestablished in these cities and regions but the persecutions, massacres, and expulsions had their intended effects by the fifteenth century of drastically reducing the number Jews and Jewish communities in Germany, and making the communities that survived smaller, poorer, more isolated, and less significant than they had been since the early centuries of settlement.

The Jewish response to these persecutions and loss of livelihood in Germany and across Europe was to look elsewhere for safety and opportunity. In the thirteenth century that elsewhere was to the east in Poland, and later, Lithuania (which at times was one with Poland). Jews fled to Poland from Germany, Austria, Hungary, England, Spain, France, and the Crimea. Over the one hundred years of the fifteenth century Poland's Jewish population grew from 15,000 to 150,000 and by the mid-sixteenth century 80 per cent of the world's Jews lived in Poland.

Like Germany, Poland was a decentralized state with power in the hands of princes and dukes who ruled the local and regional polities and cities. Some of these rulers welcomed Jews fleeing oppression in the west and afforded them legal and civil rights, religious freedom, protection from Christian-inspired persecution, and economic privileges as traders, moneylenders, accountants, tax collectors and tavern-keepers, taverns being a steady source of taxes. The appeal of the Jewish immigrants was two-fold, just as it had been and would be again several centuries later in the German states. First, Polish towns and villages had been depopulated by the Mongol invasions of the middle thirteenth century and Jews leaving Western Europe and Germany provided a large pool of men, women, and children who expanded the market for Polish farm and craft products. Second, the Polish nobility was eager to grow their economies, expand trade networks, and create orderly and efficient governments and Jews provided just the expertise and experience in commerce, finance, and accounting the nobles were looking for. By the fourteenth century and through the fifteenth Jews dominated Polish trade, with cattle, horses, and textiles their main products with their international trade networks extending to the eastern Mediterranean.

The grant of religious freedom attracted prominent rabbis and scholars who established yeshivas, making Poland and later Poland-Lithuania the world centre of Ashkenazi learning and teaching and the birthplace of the Hassidism and other movements. As with all matters, government tolerance and support was driven by its own financial interests, as Jewish tax collectors and traders provided a major portion of state income. In 1503 the Chief Rabbinate was created and the Chief Rabbi given considerable administrative and judicial control over the Jewish communities, with the backing of the government and the collaboration of local Polish councils. But, as with other freedoms, the Rabbinate was allowed primarily because it centralized the collection of taxes from the Jewish communities, with seventy percent passed on to the government and only the remaining thirty percent retained for the community.

As they had in Germany and elsewhere, Polish Jews lived apart from Poles and came to speak and write their own language, Eastern Yiddish, which morphed from the Western Yiddish brought by the Jewish German migrants. The two dialects differed primarily through the incorporation of Slavic vocabulary into the Eastern dialect, which became the major form of

Yiddish and the one brought in the nineteenth and twentieth centuries by immigrants to the United States, Britain, and elsewhere.

But, the difficult Jewish experience in Germany and elsewhere soon recurred in Poland. From the beginning Jewish traders were resented by farmers, craftsmen, and Christian traders who objected to steep interest rates, unfair competition, and especially the practice of Jews taking property as collateral on loans. Their role as tax collectors put them in the impossible position of being at odds with both the Poles from whom they collected and the nobles for whom they collected for. The former thought they took too much and the later that they took too little. And the 'protection' of the nobles only went so far as in Poland, as elsewhere, Jews were blamed for the Black Death and massacred. The hostility boiled over into anti-Jewish riots in 1407 and 1449 and the Jewish community was expelled temporarily from Cracow in 1495. More damaging to the Jewish situation were complaints about unfair trade practices that in 1485 led to Jews being barred from the craft guilds and limited their trade activities, marking a decline in the influence and wealth of the Polish Jewish community. Nonetheless, the sheer size of the Jewish population and its status as the center of Ashkenazi Judaism allowed the Polish Jewish community to retain its place as the largest and most influential into the late nineteenth century.

As Poland became less tolerant and the Jewish experience began to contract, opportunity appeared again in the West in the early sixteenth century. Jews began returning to some German states and Austria, the Netherlands afforded Jews religious freedom in 1579, and England allowed Jews to return in 1655. Nobles in these and other nations recognized the commercial expertise and international experience of Jewish traders and from the sixteenth into the eighteenth century relied on a select number of Jews, commonly labelled court Jews, for diplomatic and financial advice and their commercial skills.

Historians do not fully agree on what broader changes led Western European leaders to again welcome Jews but as was always the case, the economy was paramount. The European population was increasing following the depopulation resulting from the famines and Plague of the fourteenth century and cities were growing, creating a demand for farm and craft products. And, international trade was again expanding, creating even more demand for farm and craft products. The need was for traders who were literate, could exchange currency, travel internationally, extend credit, make loans, and negotiate. Jews, now eager to leave Poland, answered the call. At first most went to Protestant nations or Protestant regions in divided nations such as Germany whose economies were transforming more quickly, but Catholic nations and regions eventually sought their services as well.

This very brief summary of 1,200 years of Jewish life has brought us up the sixteenth century. My purpose was to mark the emergence and describe several of the key general patterns discussed in Chapter 2. In the following two chapters with these general patterns providing context, we shift our attention to the particular, the Jewish experience in rural communities with a focus on the village of Uehlfeld in Middle Franconia, Bavaria, the town where my mother's maternal ancestors lived for at least two-hundred years.

4
Uehlfeld's Secret Jewish Past

It was a clear June morning. Gazing southeast from the Jewish cemetery hill we could see the small town of Markt Uehlfeld, its houses and shops clustered together in the river valley below. Lying between our vantage point and the town were soft fields, some plowed, others dotted with delicate blue flowers. The St. Jacobus dome towered over the town's narrow streets while the River Aisch wound its way south on the far side of town. Uehlfeld is picturesque. Bicycle tourists know to stop and quench their thirst and take in the atmosphere at Brauerei Prechtel or Brauerei-Gasthof Zangzer. But we hadn't driven there from Frankfurt to enjoy the scenery or the beer, although we did find time for both. We were there to explore the Jewish history of this small town, where the Rindsberg branch of my mother's family had lived for at least 200 years.

4. The Uehlfeld cemetery in 1993. Note stones that have repaired or replaced. (Courtesy Hans Gawronski)

We didn't need a reminder, but the silent 275 or so gravestones about us provided ample evidence that the town for several centuries was home to a substantial Jewish community. Older stones were inscribed in Hebrew, more recent ones in German and Hebrew. Those that were still legible told us the names of a sizeable number of the town's former Jewish families, many of our Rindsberg ancestors among them. We were gratified to find these remains of the former Jewish community. The town itself had had no living Jewish residents since 1956. When we had strolled about town before driving out to the cemetery, we had seen nothing that told us of the town's Jewish heritage. If we had been uninterested visitors, content to just take in Uehlfeld's charm and beer, we would have driven off, never knowing that Uehlfeld was home to a Jewish community for over 400 years. Although we knew why the cemetery was the only survivor, it was troubling that it was the only survivor, especially since the Uehlfeld Jewish community had been a large one, constituting nearly half the town's population for several decades in the nineteenth century. It was also an influential community, the district rabbinate for much of that same century and served by two influential Reform rabbis, Samson Wolf Rosenfeld and Isaac Loewi.

Using the genocidal and now obsolete lexicon of Nazi Germany, Uehlfeld in 1992 was *Judenfrei,* that is, free of Jews. In 1956 the last resident of full Jewish parentage died; the fifteen or so still hanging on in 1938 had been driven out by that December. The outside walls of the synagogue remain, the structure rebuilt after the Second World War as a farm products and equipment warehouse, and the former Jewish school now houses government offices. Two decades later, in 2015, there was still no signage to tell visitors of the former Jewish community, that the farm products warehouse was once the ornate synagogue, a source of pride not just for the Jewish community but also for the entire town. The three- and four-story homes of the former Jewish families pressed up close to Raiffeisenstrasse and other streets in the former Jewish neighbourhood remain, now the modernized homes of German families.

To find no Jewish residents in Uehlfeld in 1992 and again in 2015 was hardly surprising in Germany or across much of central and eastern Europe. Thousands of Jewish communities were destroyed during the Nazi era, and very few have reappeared, and when they have, they are in cities with far fewer residents than in the past. Uehlfeld was just one of some 1,600 Jewish communities destroyed in Germany alone. Yet, while towns like Uehlfeld no longer have any Jewish residents, they still have their Jewish histories and might also have visible reminders of that history, most often a cemetery, but also memorial monuments, plaques, stones and historic markers and, as in Uehlfeld, the synagogue repurposed for secular use. The town of Adelsdorf, about fifteen miles from Uehlfeld, as one nearby example among several, erected a marble monument in 1997 to its Jewish citizens killed in the Holocaust. Uehlfeld, however, has yet to erect such markers. This too is not unusual in Germany, but not nearly as unusual as it once was. For the past twenty-five years or so, a growing number of German communities like Adelsdorf have been recognizing their former Jewish communities and residents by erecting or allowing to be erected monuments of various types including memorials to Jews who were killed in the Holocaust and historic markers at the sites of their synagogues burned on *Kristallnacht*. In Uehlfeld the only reminder of the Jewish community in 2015 is the Jewish cemetery, now protected by the high wall and sturdy metal gate, having been reconstructed after the Second World War by local people, under orders of the occupying American military.

Despite the absence of visual reminders of the town's Jewish past and apparently little interest by the town's government in creating any, we do know a good deal about Uehlfeld's Jewish heritage. We know because a relatively large and deep written record survives in local and regional and church archives. That we have this record at all is largely due to the diligent record keeping of several hundred years of government officials and Lutheran pastors who, ironically, in part because of their dislike of their Jewish neighbors, kept a close watch on the Jewish community. Pastors recorded how many Jews lived there and from 1706 on kept a census of Jewish households, listing the given names of the heads of household. They usually obtained their information about the Jewish community from the rabbi or school teacher who kept their own records. District records kept in the larger towns and cities of Bamberg, Dachsbach, Neustadt, and Bayreuth tell us about property transfers, protection taxes, and most anything else that could be taxed, including circumcisions and musicians performing at marriage ceremonies. Also filed away were reports of crimes, expulsions and returns, protection agreements (*schutzbrief*), and decrees affecting the community or its individual members. Civil records reporting births, marriages, and deaths are available only from the late eighteenth century on and are details supplied often by the pastor, again based on reports he received from the rabbi or the school teacher. Reports on the German residents are equally detailed, and comparing the two provides a sense of the ways in which Jewish and German life differed or were alike.

I have selected Uehlfeld as our focal town for rural Jewish life because one-half of my mother's family history played out over some 200 plus years in Uehlfeld and the nearby town of Burghaslach. Her Rindsberg and Sturm ancestors settled in these two towns in the early 1700s, or perhaps even earlier, and continued to live there over the next seven generations until the last few were driven out by the Nazis in 1938.

Uehlfeld, officially Markt Uehlfeld, is a small market town located in the Aisch River Valley (*Aischgrund*) in the Middle Franconia administrative district of Bavaria. The town was probably first established in the 6th century by Franks moving east as an agricultural community. The territory of what is today Middle Franconia from the fourteenth to the early nineteenth centuries was divided up among several small political units including margraviates, free cities, and the church-owned territory. For several centuries the margraves who ruled from Ansbach, Brandenburg, and Bayreuth (these holdings were sometimes united and sometimes split apart) ruled parts of the region, including Uehlfeld. Late in the eighteenth century the territory was sold to Prussia, and then, between 1803 and 1817 Eastern Franconia, which included Middle Franconia and adjacent regions was incorporated into the Kingdom of Bavaria, where the region remained until the German states unified in 1871, although the Kingdom of Bavaria was not officially abolished until 1921.

The nobles who ruled the region held the title of margrave, a noble rank between count and a duke. At one time, margraves commanded large armies, but after the Thirty Years' War their military role diminished and they functioned much as other landholding nobles of lower or higher rank. Nobles owned various amount of land as well as towns and two or more nobles might even own different sections of the same town, or in Uehlfeld's case, the town at times fell into two different administrative districts. Further complicating the political situation was that margraves acquired additional holdings, divided or disposed of holdings, and also passed these on to their heirs, meaning that new rulers periodically took over, creating uncertainty in the Jewish community about whether or not protection agreements with the former ruler would be honored by the new one. Regardless of who the noble was and his rank, protection meant that Jews lived there at the noble's pleasure. The noble decided how many Jews could live there and what occupations they could have, could issue new rules governing their behavior, and could expel them when he pleased. If the noble's territory came under the control of a larger political entity such as a principality, other policies affected how Jews were treated as well. Nevertheless, because Germany was made up of hundreds of small political units, much authority usually rested with the local or district ruler. It thus was the margrave who approved the construction of Jewish community institutions such as the school and also approved the hiring of the rabbi. Lesser Jewish religious specialists such as the cantor, teacher, and *shochet* were selected by the community.

In the Middle Ages Uehlfeld was protected by a stone wall, with residents living and keeping their livestock and harvest within the safety of the wall at night and planting their crops and grazing their livestock during the day in the fields and meadows beyond. That protection is now long gone and no longer needed; all that remains is the imposing half-timber entrance tower. The wall did not always provide enough protection. The town was devastated by several major fires and wars, the most damaging being the Thirty Years' War (1618 – 1648), which sent Uehlfelders fleeing to cities following a massacre and torching in 1632, leaving behind only 31 people from a population of more than 600. At the direction of the margrave, the few Jewish families fled up the Aisch to Höchstadt where they were sheltered by Jewish families.

After the war, which left a third of continental Europe in ruins and especially damaged Germany, the town recovered under the leadership of its Lutheran pastor, Veit von Berg; celebrated today as the modern town's founder, with a street and two schools named in his honor. But the population increased only slowly over the next three centuries, reaching just 850 in 1924. Substantial growth came only after the Second World War, from which the town escaped undamaged and then benefitted from reconstruction projects. In 2015 it had nearly 3,000 residents. The most recent expansion has been largely through the building of tract housing on the edges of the town, which has left the town centre – the old town – as it has been for centuries, with stone, stucco and half-timber buildings and the Haupstrasse lined with small shops. Agriculture is no longer important, and most of the small family farms outside town are gone. Uehlfeld is now home to several small regional businesses, to shops and to commuters.

Because my mother's family had lived there for two centuries or more and some still lived there in the 1920s and 1930s, my mother knew Uehlfeld very well. Her grandfather, David Rindsberg, was one of the last of what had been many dozens of Rindsberg kin to live in Uehlfeld. All Rindsberg descendants still living in Uehlfeld in the 1930s traced their ancestry to a man named Feist who was born in Uehlfeld in the mid-1700s. We do not know if he was the first Rindsberg ancestor to settle in Uehlfeld. It may have been Feist's father or a man we think was named Meier or perhaps Meier's father, or even someone else further back in time. But it was not likely that anyone was there before 1632 when only one Jewish family lived in town. We do know that whoever the first Uehlfelder Rindsberg was, he did not go by the surname Rindsberg. The surname came into use in 1818, when all Jews in Uehlfeld first took surnames. Records kept over the centuries by the town's rabbis, Lutheran pastors and the district administrators show that the ancestors of the three sons of Feist who in 1818 started calling themselves

Rindsberg lived in Uehlfeld in the early 1700s. Given the paucity of early records and difficulty tracing Jewish individuals before Jewish surnames came into use in town, we'll likely never know when the first ancestor arrived or who he or she was. As we said, the first man we know was a Rindsberg ancestor was a man recorded on the list of 'protected' Jews in Uehlfeld in 1767 as Feist Meier. Feist was born in Uehlfeld in about 1740 and died there in about 1820. Feist was his given name, Meier was his father's given name. Jewish men were typically identified by their first name and sometimes also the name of their father; the Jewish form would have been Feist *ben* Meier, meaning 'Feist, son of Meier'. In official records they were usually listed by their first name followed by their father's first name, or sometimes *Jud or Jude*, German for Jew.

We were eager to find ancestors before Feist Meier, but our efforts educated us in the tantalizing possibilities and frustrations of Jewish genealogy. As I said, Jewish residents of Uehlfeld were tracked carefully in town and district records. Since our ancestor was named Feist Meier we knew that his father was named Meier. In the 1706 census of the Jewish population (the first for the town that lists the men's given names) duly reported by the pastor, we found a 'Meyer Jud' with a wife and one son and daughter. There are no other men named Meyer among the twenty-three listed. So, this Meyer may be the father of Feist Meier, although we can't be sure, since there is no record of the latter's birth or parentage.

Uehlfeld, like Bavaria, is captivating. One cannot help but be drawn to the azure skies, green forests; flower-flecked fields; ragged stork nests on rooftops, the narrow streets and the half-timber homes. But the Jewish experience in Uehlfeld or Franconia in general had little to do with what entices tourists today. Over the centuries after Jews first settled there in about 1500, Jewish life was about family, building their community, buying and selling, paying taxes, praying, education, protection, persecution, expulsion, immigration and emigration, and then, for only some fifty years, citizenship and opportunity, and finally twenty-five of a downward spiral of persecution, expulsion and death.

The first Jewish families arrived in the Franconia region in the fifteenth and sixteenth centuries. Most of the early settlers came from Upper and Lower Bavaria and Upper Palatinate, from where they had been expelled. Franconia was not a politically unified region so the usually small Jewish communities lived under the rule of the various nobles, church officials, and city councils whose primary interest in allowing them to remain was financial. Jewish lives were restricted in various ways well into the nineteenth century. Limits were placed on where they could live and on how many could live there. In a pattern common across Germany, they were forced into supporting themselves mainly by trading, peddling, and lending money, imperilled by attacks on their religion, massacred or expelled several times, and generally treated as outcasts who adhered to a religion abhorrent to their Christian neighbours, who regarded Jews as the murderers of Jesus and treated them accordingly, with a shifting mixture of indifference, distrust and hostility. In addition, by this time in German history, a strong sense of German identity had taken hold, resting in part on physical and emotional ties to the land and farming – working the soil – and as British historian Neil McGregor notes: 'The German attachment to the forest is still there, as old as the hills, or at least as the oaks, a central part of the national character' (p. 128). Jews, given their centuries of trading and money lending, were clearly not a people of the soil and did not share in this identity. Jewish identity was based on their religion and their occupations. Because they were few in number, allowed to reside in a town for the financial benefit of the ruler, and despised by the church, Jewish families and entire communities came and went over the centuries from many towns. Nonetheless, there were always Jewish communities in Franconian towns and cities just as there were in other regions of Germany until the 1930s.

If the many histories of the Jewish people tell us anything about the Jewish diaspora, it is that for some 2,000 years Jews have lived where they had an opportunity to make a living and where they were permitted to live. In Chapter 3 we saw this pattern playing out in Germany on and off for some 1,200 years and Jewish settlement in Franconia was no different. As elsewhere, the opportunity was economic as Jews could make a living in Franconia, mainly in its many small towns, as Jews were banned from several cities including Nuremberg and Bayreuth for several centuries. Until the twentieth century, Franconia was farm country, with hops for beer making and corn, fruit, wheat, cattle, and dairy products its major products. Jewish traders and moneylenders found a place as middlemen, traveling about selling the hops, cattle, and other products produced by the peasant farmers and lending money to both their German suppliers and customers. Taxes and fees on Jews, their activities, and their institutions provided substantial income for the princes, margraves, and other nobles who owned the land, since Jewish taxes were heavier than those paid by Christians. The second part of the settlement equation, permission, was that Jews came to Franconia because, as we noted, they were driven out of other places in Germany and Europe and some local Franconian rulers offered them protection. Once settled in Franconia, the community itself could not simply relocate although individual members could and marriage customs in which the bride took her dowry and moved to the husband's community, and inheritance customs in which only one child inherited the father's property made such individual relocations fairly common. Establishing a community did not mean long-term stability, as we have seen Jewish communities were expelled and then readmitted any number of times from many communities. But individuals and families usually somewhere else to settle as other nobles would recruit them to their towns to meet their need for Jewish money lending and trading services and taxes. Franconian Jews did not have the option of mass emigration from the region (again, opportunity and permission) until the mid-1800s, when as part of the mass German immigration to America, they quickly took advantage, heading to freedom and opportunity across the Atlantic.

In addition to acceptance and economic opportunity, Jewish Germans, as with all marginal peoples, preferred living in some communities as opposed to others also for personal reasons. The historical record has little to say about this because their Christian rulers who kept the records had limited interest in the inner workings of their Jewish communities, but we can safely assume that a desire to live with other Jews was a consideration in where Jews chose to live. Judaism not only separated them from Christians but was the basis of Jewish community solidarity, made possible family and community support, and possibly even meant some safety in numbers. German Jews were endogamous – they married only other Jews – so living near other Jewish families ensured that parents could find suitable mates for their sons and daughters, although many marriages were to women or men from other communities. Adhering to *Halakha* (Jewish law) required the establishment and maintenance of their religious institutions – synagogue, cemetery, school, *mikvah* – and the presence of religious specialists – rabbi, cantor, *shochet*, teacher, kosher butcher – and it took a community of sufficient number (at least ten adult men) and wealth to build and sustain these institutions and occupations. Few communities had a resident rabbi and instead as Jewish communities became more numerous nearby ones were aggregated into a regional and/or district rabbinate, typically seated in a town with a large Jewish population like Uehlfeld in the 1800s or a city like Baeirsdorf or Fürth.

Especially important to the Jewish community was having a *minyan* (the ten adult men required for the prayer service). All Jewish men over age thirteen qualified including residents, visitors, and beggars and sometimes an under-age boy might be allowed if the minyan was one man short. Other considerations that might draw a family to a specific town were prior economic relations such as cooperation in cattle dealing, a previous economic relationship with local farmers, a former common place of residence, kinship ties, and friendship.

By 1524 Jews were reportedly living in Uehlfeld. The first Jewish residents of Uehlfeld and nearby towns were apparently encouraged to settle there around 1500 by Anna (1437-1512), the Electress of Saxony, by birth, and of Brandenburg, by marriage to Margrave Albrecht Achilles (1414 - 1486), the ruler of Brandenburg and Ansbach. Albrecht and Anna had built a fortress ten miles down the Aisch in Neustadt and she kept her court there after Albrecht's death, with two of his sons, Frederick I and Siegmund, ruling his former realms. Some of these first Jewish settlers probably came from nearby Nuremberg following the expulsion of its Jewish residents in 1499. The expulsion was meant to be permanent and no Jew was allowed back into Nuremburg for over 300 years, thereby encouraging settlement in nearby towns like Uehlfeld.

Not a great deal is known of Jewish life in these early years of settlement, since nearly all records of the community as well as the town's church records were lost when the town was burned in 1632 during the Thirty Years' War. Entries in the town's parish records from 1798 indicate a Jewish presence in town dating to the 1500s. The earliest official record indicating a Jewish community in Uehlfeld is a decree issued on 2 October 1583, by Margrave George Frederick I (1539-1603), ruler of Brandenburg-Bayreuth and Ansbach, to the *kastner* (his manager of the court treasury and collector of taxes) Paul Durrn of Dachsbach, the district office five miles south of Uehlfeld:

> In accord with Parliament's decree in AD 1564 and again afterwards, to halt the settlement of Jews because of the high usury and harm to the poor and because it is not fitting for Christian authorities to tolerate and protect Jews who mock and despise the Christian religion, promises that he as ruler commands that all the Jews and their domestic property immediately depart between now and March from the principality, country, government and territory of the Lord Marquis from any place they now live.

The Jewish community did leave, only to return and then be expelled again in 1613, when, again invoking the 1583 decree, Christians were prohibited from doing business with Jews. The ban was lifted in 1619, and a few Jewish families returned to Uehlfeld and then soon fled with most of Uehlfeld's residents in 1632 during the Thirty Years' War. The town's pastor recorded six protected Jews in town at the time, 'Wolf Jud, Amstel Jud, Amstel Meier, Mosch Jud, Marx Jud, Gümblein Jud' and two protected in Uehlfeld but living in Neustadt, 'old Berla Jud, Jacob Jud.' The total Jewish population he estimated at between forty and fifty, the majority being children. Margrave Christian Ernst (1644-1712), like other rulers in the region, began to rebuild the town by welcoming Protestants from Austria, French Huguenots and displaced Jews as well as Jewish families fleeing west from persecution in Eastern Europe. By 1685 the town was home to four protected Jews, two of them, Marx Jud and Wolf Jud, very likely men who had fled in 1632. The nearby town of Schornweisach had three more. All paid an annual protection tax of 5 fl., except for 'old' Samuel who paid only 1 fl. Franconia was on its way to having a mixed Protestant-Catholic population with a small minority of Jews. Middle Franconia was to become the most Protestant district, with about 75 per cent of the population Protestant and 2 per cent Jewish.

The Jewish settlement of small towns and Jewish life in those towns was often influenced by court Jews who served the ruling noble. Court Jews is a generic label for Jewish men who served nobles in Germany and other European nations as financial advisors, bankers, trade representatives, managers of the currency, and suppliers to the military. A few were also permitted to operate as industrialists and merchants trading in tobacco, textiles, and jewelry. Court Jews had greater freedom than other Jews including paying taxes at the lower Christian rate, competing equally in the marketplace, and sometimes living in places where other Jews were not permitted. Because of their status and wealth and access to the ruler, they often represented the Jewish community in the territory and sought to forestall expulsions, encouraged the return of Jews following expulsion, funded synagogues and cemeteries and advocated for increased rights for Jews.

Uehlfeld was too small to have court Jews, but Jews were no doubt drawn to the town in the late 1600s and early 1700s in part because of the influence of Samson Solomon (also known as Samson Solomon Baiersdorf) a court Jew to Margrave Chrsitian Ernst from 1670 until Solomon's death in 1712. Solomon lived in Baiersdorf, the locale of the margrave's summer court as Jews had been barred from living in Bayreuth, the locale of the court, since 1515 and did not return in large numbers until the middle 1700s. Over his forty years of service Solomon was the most influential court Jew in Ernst's court and probably the most influential court Jews in all of southern Germany. Solomon expanded his service into a family business; his two sons were also court Jews as was a son-in-law and the son-in-law's brother. Such family and dynastic of court Jews were not unusual, two especially influential ones being the Oppenheimers in Vienna and the Rothchilds in Frankfurt.

Samson was instrumental in making Uehlfeld and other towns in the margravaite more attractive to Jewish settlers and life a bit easier for them. Most importantly, in 1695 he encouraged Margrave Ernst to give Jews freedom of trade. In 1709, with the margravaite now encompassing several towns like Uehlfeld, Burghaslach, Erlangen, and Baiersdorf with substantial

Jewish populations, Samson and his fellow court Jews formed a Jewish council to oversee Jewish affairs. They established the rabbinate in Baiersdorf, selected the chief rabbi, controlled the influx of 'foreign' Jews, encouraged settlement in Baiersdrof, and established two cemeteries. Solomon himself funded the building a new synagogue in Baiersdorf to serve the expanding community.

Despite their wealth, prestige and influence, a court Jew's status was precarious, resting on the support of the noble and also the diplomatic skills of the court Jew in negotiating the intrigues of the noble's court. Thus, a court Jew could lose his position if the noble became disenchanted with his performance, the court Jew made enemies in the court, or the noble died and his heir preferred someone else. Solomon and his sons experienced but survived some of these difficulties. Solomon himself nearly lost his position when embroiled in a court intrigue with an influential advisor to the margrave. Fortunately, Solomon's rival was the one who lost the power struggle, allowing Solomon to maintain his influence. Later his two sons encountered more serious difficulty when they complained to the territorial council that the margrave had not paid them a large debt. The margrave struck back and they found themselves on trial and then imprisoned, freed only when they agreed to forego the claimed debt and to make no future claims on the margrave.

Despite their economic role as middlemen, even small number of Jews displeased local church officials. One who frequently made his displeasure known was Uehlfeld's pastor Johann Laubenter who objected to the margrave's re-settlement initiative, leading him to complain in 1686 that 'this place in time will become a right Sodom and Gomorrah and Jewish town'. The margrave, needing Jewish traders and their taxes, ignored the pastor's warning and continued to encourage Jewish settlement. Laubenter's complaint reflected Christian hostility to Jews and concern about the size and influence of the Jewish community. A pastor's complaints were not always just motivated by religion as sometimes the pastor was representing the interests of Christian craftsmen and merchants who sought to remove Jewish competitors and also by peasants who complained about Jewish business practices in which they accused Jewish traders of charging exorbitant interest rates on loans and colluding to set high interest rates or keep what they paid the farmers for their products low. Following the pattern established centuries earlier, Jews were also scapegoated for all and any difficulties that befell the peasants – human and animal disease, crop failures, poverty, storms, and so on. Jewish communities did not simply accept expulsion orders nor the violence that sometimes accompanied them, and would negotiate with the local noble to halt the expulsion, now and again succeeding when they agreed to pay higher taxes. Sometimes the threat of expulsion was simply a ruse to get Jews to pay more taxes or to forgive debts.

As we have seen, Christian-based hostility to and restrictions on Jewish communities goes back to the time that Christianity first arrived in western Germany in the late fourth century CE. In Middle Franconia, which was mainly Protestant by the time Jewish communities became established, Lutheran (Evangelical) pastors were following the judgments and advice of Martin Luther set forth in his *The Jews & Their Lies* in 1543. In a change from the tolerance he offered earlier, Luther now, among other actions, recommended that nobles expel all Jews under their rule and that Christians burn their synagogues, raze their houses, confiscate their prayer books, and force Jews to live in communal shelters and do manual labour. Because the noble often wanted a Jewish community of traders, pastors could often not keep Jews out or have them expelled, so instead worked to limit the size and growth and influence of the Jewish population in their towns. Toward this end, pastors often included information about the Jewish community in their periodic reports to the margrave and, beginning in 1706, in Uehlfeld, a census. The pastoral reports discussing their Jewish community are littered with adjectives and nouns such as *rotten, scum* or *pigs*. Some clergy did all they could to hamper the growth and stability of the Jewish community. In the 1700s and 1800s, Uehlfeld's pastors fought unsuccessfully against the building of the synagogue and the Jewish school. As mentioned, their expulsion requests were often ignored by the margrave who was more interested in his treasury and also in balancing the economic interests of the German farmers and the Jewish traders, both of whom were the vital players in the local and regional economies. To keep the pastors satisfied, though, the margraves were more receptive to calls for more restrictions (often economic) on the Jewish community, short of expulsion.

We get some sense of this dynamic among the pastors, the margraves and the Jewish communities from an account of an incident in Uehlfeld in 1707. The incident centred on one of the town's many fires, and the key participants were Pastor M. Joh. Gross (who also submitted all or part of the report), the Jewish school teacher Tobias Levi who had lived in town for four years with his wife and two children, and Margrave George Frederick Karl (1688 - 1735). The incident played out as follows. In October 1707 a large crowd of spectators, including many Jewish residents, gathered to watch a fire raging at the town's mill. The mill was perhaps the town's most important building and the miller one of the wealthiest residents. Tobias Levi joined the crowd and after surveying the situation, took it upon himself to employ Jewish rituals to extinguish the fire. He requested a loaf of unleavened bread and when one could not be found accepted instead a leavened loaf from the miller. Upon receiving the bread, he held it in his hand and wrote in chalk the letter V in several spots in front of the fire, and as he circled the fire he prayed out loud, reciting from *Numbers* 11:2: 'And the people cried unto Moses; and when Moses prayed unto the Lord, the fire was quenched.' He then had Hans Sitten, a man from nearby Demantsfurth, toss the bread into the conflagration, selecting Sitten because he was strong. Levi's intervention seemed to help; the fire died down, the letter Vs disappeared, and the bread was reportedly found only half-burned the next morning.

Pastor Gross was outraged, writing to Margrave Karl that Levi employed 'cabbalistic' practices and also publicly invoked the supposed special relationship between Jews and God, thereby questioning the primacy of Christianity. The pastor was correct in labeling the Levi's rituals 'cabbalistic' as the use of magical letters and the sacrifice of bread was firmly in the tradition of Kabbalah, or mystical Judaism, popular at the time in much of Europe. The following year, when called to testify about his actions, Levi noted that his actions were in accord with Jewish custom, as Jews did the same in Fürth and Prague and around the world. Plus, he noted that he had employed the same rituals to help extinguish a fire in nearby Erlangen, another town under Karl's rule.

Margrave Karl ordered an inquiry, which included having two of his officials question Levi. Fortunately, the transcript of the interview remains in the district archive and the questions put to Levi provide insight into Jewish-Christian relations and Christian concerns about the growing Jewish population in town. Several questions gave Levi the opportunity to describe the rituals he carried out –what he said, what he wrote and what those words meant to him. He recounted what he did but could offer little in explaining the meaning of what he did or said, pointing out that he lacked the requisite education and such matters were better answered by rabbis. His interrogators were especially interested in the loaf of bread, where it came from, how it got in the fire, and if he paid for it. He gave them the facts as noted above and answered he had no knowledge of whether the loaf burned or not as he had not gone back to look. Finally, the officials got to the heart of the matter: whether Levi was denigrating Christianity and seeking to attract Christian townsfolk to Judaism. Levi denied the suggestion that he had claimed that his methods, and especially the use of bread, was superior to all other methods. More to the point, they asked if the letter he had written meant that: "The Gentile God is not a God"? He responded that "he knew nothing about it and also said that in his law he had not heard such a thing in his lifetime." Finally, he noted that the miller had not paid him for his help and in fact had not even thanked him.

A year later (a time period the pastor found much too long) Margrave Karl ordered Levi to stop engaging in superstitious behaviour, threatened physical action if he continued and ordered him to pay for any damages caused by his actions. Our understanding of the incident and pastor Gross's and Margrave Karl's reactions is aided by considering the temporal context. As we saw, in the early 1700s, the town was still being re-populated following the Thirty Years' War and the pastor saw the growing Jewish community as a threat to the still small Protestant community. The margrave saw it differently as he welcomed Jews for their trading acumen and taxes, so he was slow to respond to the pastor's complaint and was lenient with Levi who performed a valuable function as the teacher to the Jewish community.

The earliest count of the Jewish population in Uehlfeld dates to 1632 and shows a community of forty to fifty individuals, the majority children, in a total population of about 600. The burning of the town that year reduced the population to one Jewish family. After repopulation following the Thirty Years' War, the community was about the same size as before the war, consisting of ten households and fifty individuals in 1684. The majority were again probably children, hence the opening of the school two years later. A report written by Pastor Gross to the district administrator in Dachsbach in 1706 provides the first 'official' census we have of the town's Jewish population. Jewish families accounted for 23 households and totaled 134 individuals: 24 men, 25 women, 34 sons, 44 daughters, and 8 servants. Although many in the Jewish communities were poor, there was some variation in wealth and in Uehlfeld as elsewhere a few families often had servants. In Uehlfeld the censuses show in 1715 three families with servants, one of them having two; in 1753 eleven households each having one servant each; and in 1763 again eleven households each with one servant and two with two servants each. Families with servants were typically wealthy (by town and rural Jewish standards) and/or had many young children. Most servants were young men or women who were willing to look after the children, cook, clean, make the fire, haul water and run errands so as to accumulate a bit of cash before they married. Households varied in size although many had more children than adults. In Uehlfeld in 1706 the smallest household was a single widow, the largest was twelve individuals headed by Fäustlein Jud, and consisting of his wife, five sons, four daughters and either his or his wife's mother.

By 1712 Uehlfeld had the largest Jewish population of the seventeen towns with Jewish communities in the margraviate. Only Baiersdorf had a larger Jewish population. The region's growing Jewish population was mostly found in small towns; the two cities of Bayreuth and Nuremburg, in fact, had no Jewish residents at all, having expelled their Jewish communities some

> Natürlich wurde nun dem Pfarrer eine Aufstellung abgefordert, wieviel Juden in Uehlfel
>
> „ Specification derjenigen Judenköpf, wie stark sie sich zu Anfang des 170(
> Pfarrei Uehlfeld befunden haben:
>
> 1. Judenschulmeister, Frau, 1 Kind, 2 Gesind — 5
> 2. Frommel Jud, Vater Marx, Frau, 4 Kinder, 1 Gesind — 8
> 3. Cohn Löb, Frau, 6 Kinder — 8
> 4. Itzig Jud, Frau, 1 Kind — 3
> 5. Scheuerlein Jud, Frau, 3 Kinder — 5
> 6. Victer Löb, Frau — 2
> 7. Löben Achtermann, Frau — 2
> 8. Pfeiffer Jud, Frau, 5 Kinder — 7
> 9. Hirsch Jud, Frau, 7 Kinder — 9
> 10. Salomon Jud, Frau, 7 Kinder — 9
> 11. Nathan Jud, Frau, 5 Kinder, 1 Gesind — 8
> 12. Jonas Jud, Frau, 2 Kinder — 4
> 13. Leiser Jude, Frau, Schwiegermutter, 4 Kinder — 7
> 14. Samuel Jud, Frau, 7 Kinder — 9
> 15. Joseph Jud, Frau, 2 Kinder — 4
> 16. Löben Scheuerlein, Frau, 2 Söhne, 1 Magd — 5
> 17. Schmuhle Jud, Frau, 1 Sohn, 1 Gesind — 4
> 18. Marxen Hirsch, Frau, 2 Söhne, 2 Töchter — 6
> 19. Schlom Jud, 1 Tochter, 1 Gesind — 4
> 20. Löben Salomon, Frau, 1 Tochter — 3
> 21. Faustlein Jud, Frau, Schwiegermutter, 5 Söhne, 4 Töchter — 12
> 22. Hirsch Jud zu Demantsfürth, Frau, 2 Kinder, 1 Gesinde — 5
> 23. Mayer Jud allda, Frau, 1 Sohn, 3 Töchter — 6

5. Uehlfeld Census, 1706.

two hundred years earlier. For the next fifty years Uehlfeld's and the region's Jewish populations remained stable, with Uehlfeld's at 137 in 1715 and 134 in 1753. The large, stable population further alarmed the town's pastors and in 1719 pastor J. Mathias wrote Margrave Karl that the town would be a peaceful and happy place except for the 'evil Jewish vermin' and suggested that it was best to destroy them, by which he probably meant expel them. Margrave Karl ignored his advice. By 1763 the population had grown to 170, the beginning of a rapid increase to 218 in 1771 and then about 250 in 1775. This late- eighteenth-century increase was likely due to the arrival of Jews fleeing persecution in Poland and Lithuania and then the 1772 first partition of the Poland-Lithuanian commonwealth among Russia and Austria and the creation of the Pale of Settlement by Russia's Catherine II. This political turmoil in Poland and Russia resulted in new restrictions on Jewish settlement there and higher taxes, forcing some Jews to look west for better opportunities in Germany.

By 1796, however, Uehlfeld's Jewish population had dropped to 176. It's not clear why the population decreased but one factor may have been new regulations issued in the 1780s that further restricted Jewish economic activity. These new restrictions prohibited Jewish children from purchasing items in shops unless accompanied by a parent or other adult; required that contracts with 'smaller' people, meaning peasants, be reviewed by a government official to make sure the Jewish creditor had not placed secret conditions on the German debtor; and limited the Jewish trade in precious metals. By the early 1800s, however, the population had increased again to 202 in 1812 and 294 in 1818, with the latter forming about one-third of the town's population. This increase may have been driven by additional immigration from Poland, following the second (1793) and third (1795) partitions of the nation.

Before the 1800s Jews in many small towns lived in their own neighborhoods or streets (*Judengasse*) although they did not face the restrictions on movement of those living in cities with Jewish ghettos such as Frankfurt and Worms and in some cities and larger towns some wealthy families lived outside the Jewish neighborhood. These were typically the court Jews whose service to the noble allowed them various privileges, including living where they choose or near the noble's castle. The Jewish neighborhood in Uehlfeld was in the southern section of town, bordered by the Haupstrasse and the River Aisch. Many Jews lived on the square of streets formed by Raiffeisenstrasse, Kirchenstrasse, and Goethestrasse. The synagogue and Jewish school were on Raiffeisenstrasse and Kirchenstrasse. Once the emancipation process began in the early 1800s, some families moved to other areas of town, and later in the century several Jewish families lived on the Haupstrasse, near the town gate, perhaps the town's most desirable residential street.

In Chapter 2 I introduced 'protection', the political and economic arrangement through which each noble or church official ruled the Jewish families and communities in his or her realm. Protection emerged on a wide scale in the ninth century and remained in use into the nineteenth. Here we look at protection in more detail in rural communities. Protection came in the form of a letter or writ, the *Schutzbrief*, (also called in some locales *Geleitsbrief* or *Patent*) given by the ruler to a single Jew, usually a man but sometimes a woman (often a widow) when they first settled in the community. In many communities, only one son could inherit his father's protection and widows could and often did inherit their deceased husband's protection, especially when they also inherited his property, thereby reassuring the ruler that they had financial assets and could pay their taxes. Widows with property often re-married men from other communities, who then had to pay a reception fee when they moved to the wife's community and also annual protection taxes of their own. A community of protected Jews were categorized as *Schutzjuden*; those without *Schutzbrief* as *unvergeleitete Juden*. In some communities, especially in the north, there might be two or three categories of the protected Jews in a town or a city, with each extended a different set of rights and restrictions.

The *Schutzbrief* document, handwritten in German by a noble's agent, varied in length from a paragraph to several pages and might cover a whole range of obligations and restrictions concerning the duration of residence; amount of reception fee and annual protection tax (*Schutzgeld*); marriages of children; inheritance of the protection; travel; occupation; and trading territory. The conditions attached to protection were set by the nobleman, sometimes unilaterally, other times through negotiation with the protected Jewish man or woman. Delineating the holder's occupation was especially important to the ruler as a major purpose of affording Jews protection was to have their services as traders to sell the peasant's agricultural products. Having an occupation desirable to the ruler such as hops trader or tanner or butcher also benefited the 'protected' Jewish man as it made him a valuable economic resource and thereby afforded him a reasonable expectation that he could live out his life in the community and his son as well, so long as the son carried on the same work.

The reception fees and annual protection tax payments were a major source of not always reliable income for the ruler's treasury and their amount varied from place to place and tended to increase over time. In the mid-1700s in Uehlfeld the reception fee was 30 fl. or 60 fl. for 'foreign' Jews, meaning Jews who came from a territory ruled by a different noble. During that same period, the annual tax was 12 fl. The following extract from the tax list for 1739 for taxes paid to the Dachsbach office shows that accounting was careful and the amount due prorated when required:

> Abraham Marx. Samuel Samson. Eleasar Samson. Loser Low. Hirsch Schmul. Schuel Bonheim. Esaias Weyl (reduced according to account of 1721). Isaac Weyl. Suftlein Salomom. The Jewish schoolmaster. Izig Pfeiffer. Wolff Benjamin. Pfeiffer Low. Reichel widow of Jew Michel. Hirsch Salomon. Isaac Hecht. Issa Loser Samuel's son. Isaac Hirschbrucker. Simon Selligmann. Joseph Salomon. Samuel Baruch. Meyer Jew. Wolff Hirsch in Uehlfeld from 28 Apr. 1738 onwards. Samuel Pfeiffer from 18 Dec. 1736 onwards. Widow Beerlin is to decide whether she will pay protection fee or move away.

The *Schutzbrief* was renewed each year, although it seems to have been renewed automatically most of the time by the timely payment of the annual protection tax and the taxpayer being considered a person of 'good character'. Individuals who could not pay such as the elderly or sick usually had their tax paid by the Jewish community or the government waived or reduced the amount or extended the payment period. Reflecting the value placed on education, the teacher's tax was often waived so long as he taught that year. In small, poor Jewish communities, the margrave might collect no taxes at all. For example, in 1771 there were six towns in the Bayreuth margraviate with small Jewish communities (three to eleven families each), with community assets ranging from only 500 fl. to nearly 12,000 fl. In that year, no protected individual in any of these six towns paid a protection tax. In contrast, the margrave could count on hefty payments from town's with larger populations and more assets. That same year, Uehlfeld's 36 protected Jews, with total assets of over 25,000 fl. paid a total protection tax of 244 fl. and Bayreuth, the seat of the margraviate, with sixty-five protected Jews and assets exceeding 151,000 fl. paid 695 fl. Bayreuth's Jewish assets and taxes were so great because several wealthy court Jews who served the margrave now lived there, Jews having been permitted to return about thirty years earlier, ending some three centuries of banishment.

Beginning in the middle of the eighteenth century, *Schutzbrief* were sometimes given to an entire Jewish community and in order to control expansion, might set a limit on the Jewish population, on the number of marriages each year, and also on how many dwellings Jews could own or occupy.

If a man or woman was not protected, he or she could not live in the town and laws often limited the amount of time they could remain in town. Officials sometimes looked the other way when unprotected people (transients and beggars) lived in town, so long as they caused no trouble and the Jewish community supported them. Hospitality toward Jewish travelers was usual, Jewish traders staying in Jewish homes or inns owned by Jews which catered to Jewish travelers and provided them with kosher meals. Through their travels and overnight stays, traders created ties between families and were an important medium for news from the outside world as well as for regional gossip.

Protection was more than just about money and property and religious rights; it was one key element and a legal element in a broad complex of beliefs, attitudes and actions toward Jews which included the Church's hostility, preventing Jewish assimilation, keeping Jews as an outcaste group, limiting the size of their communities, and barring them from competing economically with Germans, holding political office, marrying non-Jews, and becoming members of German society. For the Jewish communities, protection, however burdensome its taxes, defined their relationship with the ruler and allowed them to remain in the town or city and build and maintain their community. But, because it was at the sole discretion of the ruler, being 'protected' hardly afforded a sense of security or inclusion.

In this first chapter on rural Jewish life I have fleshed out the details of several major elements of Jewish life – settlement patterns and population trends, church-Jewish community relations, and ruling noble–protected Jew relations – which provided a largely externally-controlled framework for the Jewish experience in villages and small towns. In the next chapter we remain in Uehlfeld but shift our gaze inward, to explore the inner workings of Jewish communities – housing, work, home life, worship, law and order, communal life, education and death.

5

Small Town Life

If you thing can be said about Jewish life in rural Germany it is that Jews worked very hard. To house and feed themselves, support their poor and sick, build and sustain their institutions, raise dowries for their daughters, and pay their taxes and fees, many men worked six days a week, spent much of their time walking from town to town negotiating with sellers and buyers, while praying three times each day and saving the Sabbath for prayer and reflection. Women worked equally hard and because they had many children they were often pregnant or caring for several infants and children while cooking, sewing, cleaning, preparing for the Sabbath, cleansing in the *mikvah*, shopping at the weekly market, among other routine tasks. The leaders of the community maintained the synagogue, school, and cemetery and conducted the services as few communities had a resident rabbi, adjudicated disputes, and negotiated on the community's behalf with the town or district officials. And all these tasks were carried out every day and week and month in a political, economic, and religious environment whose rules were made and enforced by the margrave and the pastor, the former interested in them mainly for the income they produced for him, and the latter eager to usher them out the gate.

But it is misleading to simply accept that Jewish village life was just about work and prayer with men and women too busy with those to do much else. There was far more to Jewish community life. Unfortunately, we do not know as much about Jewish community life as we would like, especially for the years before 1700. Just a fragment of what we do know comes from the Jewish community itself, whose records were often destroyed; much more comes from government administrative records documenting property transfers, tax payments, births, deaths, inheritances, marriages, crimes and the movement of people in and out of villages. Taken together, the details in these records of who was coming and who was going create the impression of Jewish communities in substantial motion, both on a daily basis (except on the Sabbath) and over time. And while it was true that the membership of the community fluctuated as people moved out and in, many communities like Uehlfeld had a stable core of families descended from men and women who first settled there several generations earlier. The synagogue – whether

6. FränkischeDorfjuden, 1817. Oil painting of Jews in rural Franconia in 1817. (Courtesy of the Leo Baeck Institute, New York)

a building or a room in a house – was the heart of the community, not just a place for prayer three times a day, on the Sabbath and holidays, but also as a meeting venue for the various social and charitable groups attached to it. It was also a very visible and loud (during services) symbol of the community's existence. The noise came from the men praying and also from arguments and even fights. The cemetery was the community's link to its past and, unfortunately, a place of frequent gatherings as death was a regular visitor in late medieval and early modern Europe.

There was a lot of motion in town beyond the coming and going to and from assemblies at the synagogue and cemetery. Traders, peddlers, and beggars were always on the move, walking or riding in their wagons from town to town and house to house. And, because families were dispersed across several towns, Jewish families often traveled to visit relatives. Women's work was not just in the home as they and their children fetched water and firewood, shopped and gossiped at the weekly or bi-weekly markets, cleansed in the *mikvah*, visited in others homes, shared baking ovens, and midwifed the births of each other's children. Beyond the synagogue services, families and the community celebrated at the bris and marriage ceremonies, and mourned together at funerals and during *shiva*.

Jewish life resembled that of their Christian German neighbours in some ways. Both worked hard and for long hours, although the men at different tasks. Many in both communities were poor or just managed in good times and struggled in harsher ones. The lives of both were shaped in important ways by decisions made by the margrave and the church, although the Germans had more influence, and especially the craftsmen or farmers, each group sometimes banding together to advocate for economic reforms, often including restrictions on Jewish traders or craftsmen. And both Jews and Germans shared a common trade language and norms of social interaction that allowed them to negotiate business deals and buy and sell in the markets so that both could make a living. But, their lives differed in far more meaningful ways. Germans could live where they wanted for as long as they wanted (although relocation was unusual) and they didn't need to ask for or pay for 'protection'. Only Jews need protection. Germans also paid fewer taxes, at lower rates, were exempt from some fees such as the *leibzoll* and even benefitted directly from fees paid by Jews such as those to support the Easter celebration. What mattered most of all, as it had almost always mattered most of all, was that Germans were Christians (Catholics or Lutherans, although only Lutherans in Uehlfeld).

While Judaism kept Jews apart from their Christian neighbours, it also created solidarity within the local Jewish community, with other nearby Jewish communities, with other communities in Germany and even elsewhere in Europe, West Asia and North Africa. Jews were a distinct group in Germany not just because Germans defined them as different but also because Jews, by adhering to their religion, defined themselves as different. Judaism was the core of that self-identity, reinforced through adherence to Jewish beliefs, observance of Jewish laws, performance of Jewish rituals, marriage to other Jews, and the establishment and maintenance of Jewish institutions. There were, of course, other sources of community solidarity including intermarriage between families and across towns, shared work, and friendships, but the sharing of Judaism was at the core.

Up until the late 1700s or early 1800s, depending on the region, German Jews were Orthodox (although that label only came into use in the 1800s), strictly adhering to the *Halakha* (Jewish law or Jewish path). In Uehlfeld as elsewhere, as soon as the community was large enough and could raise the funds, it would rent space for or build a synagogue, a *mikvah*, cemetery, a school and often an *eruv* (a barrier-sheltered public walkway that was defined as an extension of private space, thereby allowing men to adhere to Jewish law such as carrying items such prayer books on the Sabbath). The community had to obtain permission from the ruler to build or open their religious institutions and that permission was usually granted. Permission was not motivated, or solely motivated, by religious tolerance or altruism as indicated by the following grant of permission to Burghaslach's community:

> In 1731 the [Burghaslach] Jewish community received permission to erect four 'Schranken' [barriers] at the end of the village, as 'this will be an adornment for the market town and it was that Jewish communities in other places had recently been favored with this'. It was 'to allow Jews to carry food and drink across the street on their Sabbath according to Jewish law'. The agreement stated that the community would pay for the installation and a yearly rent of 30kr. for this, but that the upkeep would be the responsibility of the local council. (Skyte and Skyte, 2006)

Jewish communities hired their religious specialists – rabbi, cantor, teacher, kosher butcher and *shochet*. The Jewish community, not the ruler, had to raise the money to build and maintain their religious buildings and pay their religious practitioners. Only some small towns could afford or had a large enough community to sustain a synagogue and in Bavaria only a few had resident rabbis. To make sure there was rabbinical oversight, one rabbi, situated in a large town or city, served as the district rabbi for the surrounding small towns. Prayer leaders and cantors typically led the daily services. Hiring a rabbi was a serious matter. The rabbi was not only the religious leader of the community but also often represented it in negotiations with the government. Rabbis and teachers were in high demand and regional Jewish newspapers were filled with advertisements for the positions. Typical of these regular listings was one for the Uehlfeld rabbi in 1865 which promised a salary of 300 florins, an apartment in the school building, and 33 guilders to pay for heating the classroom. Rabbis and cantors were paid an annual salary by the community. In some communities cantors as with the other specialists were paid directly for their services. Serving the community in one of these positions was something of an honor and produced extra income, but also could become burdensome if it interfered with one's travels as a trader. As with other relationships involving money, religious specialists were retained via written contracts. Little was left to chance in these contracts, as shown by the detail in the following payment schedule negotiated with the cantor/shochet in Burghaslach in 1836:

1. Fixed annual cash salary 90 fl.
2. For 'calling up' on Sabbaths and Holidays from everybody 6 kr.
3. For blessing of a new mother incl. of 6 kr. For calling up 12 kr.
4. For calling up a bridegroom 24 *kr.*

5. For reading of the Megilah 1.45 fl.
6. For slaughtering of large cattle 24 kr., for a small one, calf, sheep, etc. 3 kr., for a goose 2 kr., for a chicken and a pair of pigeons 1kr. For a walk of up to one hour to slaughter outside the village 12 kr. and for each additional hour 12 kr.
7. For witnessing a signature at a wedding 1 fl. Whomever did not invite the Cantor to an engagement has to pay him compensation of 1.30 fl. The Cantor must be invited to weddings or he is to receive 3.30 fl. compensation, to be paid even if the wedding of a local son or girl was celebrated elsewhere.
8. For the writing of the engagement contract 1.30 fl. (Skyte and Skyte 2006)

Each community was part of a district and/or regional rabbinate, with the rabbinate seated in a town or city with a large Jewish population. In the 1700s Uehlfeld was in the Baiersdorf rabbinate. From 1808 until 1873 Uehlfeld was the seat of a regional rabbinate, with its rabbi overseeing the religious affairs of at first twelve and later ten communities, each of which supported the rabbinate, making a financial contribution based on its population. In 1873, for example, there were ten towns in the rabbinate, Burgambach and Geiselwind, two of the original towns, now being assigned elsewhere

Town	Number of Members	Contribution (marks)
Schornweissach	5	10.37
Pahres	15	31.50 1/2
Diespeck	44	93.21
Ullstadt	14	29.44
Scheinfeld	30	63.72
Schnarzenbach	1	23.20
Burghaslach	36	76.25
Weissendorf	11	23.20
Kairlindach	15	31.15 ½
Uehlfeld	28	59.28

Several of the larger towns like Burghaslach, Ullstadt and Scheinfeld had their own synagogues. Uehlfeld remained the rabbinate until 1873 when it was transferred to the Fürth, which had been a major centre of rabbinical thought and education and home to several wealthy and prominent Jewish merchants and financiers. Judaism has never been static, and in the late 1700s it began to change in Germany, with its new iteration, Reform Judaism, competing with and eventually largely replacing Orthodoxy, a transformation we examine in Chapter 6.

By 1696 the Uehlfeld Jewish population had grown large enough to raise sufficient funds for their first synagogue, whose establishment was allowed by Margrave Christian Ernst, the ruler who was then encouraging their settlement in town. The small synagogue was built on land in the Jewish neighbourhood adjacent to what over a century later would be the location of the new, much larger and ornate synagogue built in 1818. By 1706 the town has a resident teacher and by 1715 the community also employed a resident rabbi, a man listed in the town records as Rabbi Scheu, who lived in town with his wife and their two children. It is not known how long he remained in town but the town apparently had no resident rabbi after his departure until 1808. In 1732 the community received permission from Margrave Karl to open its cemetery, about a mile out of town on the road to Burghaslach. The cemetery was located on land purchased from Joseph Abraham, one of the community members who had used it as a vineyard. Pfeiffer Low was designated as the cemetery's first representative to the government, the property being subject to annual taxes. The land was cleared and the cemetery opened in 1734 with a wall and small mortuary added later. The cemetery was located outside town in accord with Jewish custom, which accommodated the *kohanim* (the Jewish priestly caste), who were prohibited from walking past a cemetery. In accord with Jewish requirements, the cemetery was carefully maintained by the community.

Having their own cemetery was also a great convenience as Jewish Uehlfelders no longer had to travel fifteen miles to bury their dead in the Jewish cemetery in Zeckern. Death was a regular feature of European rural life before the 1800s, with the average life expectancy being only thirty to thirty-five years and about 25 per cent of newborns dying in infancy or early childhood. Burial records from Uehlfeld show that death rate there was typical, with infants and children almost always among those dying each year. For example, in 1739 infants and children were six of the nine who were buried in the new Jewish cemetery that year:

> Two children of Wolff Hirsch in Uehlfeld who had lived for a few days only
> Levia, a foreign Jewess who visited her brother-in-law, the singer in Uehlfeld
> 19.04 Peftlein, aged 2, child of Viet David in Uehlfeld
> 19.04 Gumpel, aged 11, son of Jewish beggar Jacob in Wiesenthau
> 21.05 Izig, aged 21, son of Jewess Reichel in Uehlfeld
> 27.07 Kussel, aged 3, son of Isaac Hecht in Uehlfeld
> 30.07 Nennela, aged 5, daughter of said Isaac Hecht
> 03.12 Joseph Low in Uehlfeld

The Uehlfeld cemetery remained in use until 1937; it was vandalized before and during the Second World War, then reconstructed after the war and later afforded special protection as a Bavarian heritage site.

Cemeteries and the gravestones within them are often the oldest and only public and visible survivals of a town or city's Jewish community. Gravestones, or at least those still in one piece or legible, provide an important written record of the town's Jewish residents. Thus, cemeteries rightly draw the attention of Jewish heritage visitors and researchers. Uehlfeld's cemetery sits a bit less than a mile northwest of town on a wooded rise overlooking several hundred yards of gently rolling fields that stretch toward town. Recent housing developments have brought the town closer to the cemetery, but it's still a private, quiet place, with its high stone wall and heavy oak shade creating a sense of peace and separation from the outside world. The roughly 275 gravestones sit in clusters and rows separated by grass and trees. Surnames are still legible on many: Rindsberg, Dingfelder, Schwab, Gutherz, Himmelreich, Reichmannsdorfer, Jakob, Grabstein, Kohn, Mossman, Sturm, Schonemuller, Kleine, Rosen, Hebraish, Schwarz, Erlich, Wallish, Tuchman, Bruckheim and Selz. It is likely that the stones record the names of only a portion of the Jewish individuals buried there, as some stones were destroyed and others hauled away in the 1930s and many graves were apparently unmarked – many from the 1700s, those of beggars, infants, and children, and those of people from other towns. The small mortuary building on the grounds collapsed early in the twentieth century and was never rebuilt. In 1992 we found a pile of rubble behind the rear wall. It was mostly rough-cut, square stones from the old wall, evidently dumped there out of sight when the new wall was built.

Education (of boys) in Jewish belief and ritual was of highest import. In 1766 the community opened its first school, as recorded in an annual district report: 'The Jewish community has bought two chambers in the house of Joseph Sublein in order to establish a Jewish school.' The community received permission from the margrave to open the school and paid him a tax on the two rooms. Locating the home in one or two rooms in a house was typical of small towns which could not afford a separate building. Often as well, the school rooms were in the home of the school teacher. Teachers could not support themselves from their teaching salary alone so often held other positions, sometimes as cantor and/or *shochet*. The school remained in the two rooms until 1818 when the new synagogue opened and the adjacent old synagogue was converted into a school, which later became the public school for Jewish students in 1826. Being able to read and write mattered both for religious and business reasons. Until the 1800s, many Jewish men were literate while German peasants were usually not - Jews could read Yiddish and Hebrew and could write in Yiddish or Judeo-German while few German peasants were literate even in German.

Despite its importance, Jewish religious education before the nineteenth century in many towns was hit and miss, dependent on the presence of and the levels of interest and ability of the teacher, many of whom were busy earning additional income as the cantor, *shochet*, or butcher. When no teacher was resident, which was not unusual, religious education fell to the boys' fathers, and again, it was hit and miss. Boys probably learned more about ritual obligations from observing their father and old brothers than from class room instruction. Girls learned their religious obligations, how to cook, sew, and other female responsibilities from their mothers and older sisters and an occasional grandmother. The requisite characteristics of a 'good wife' were diligence, honesty, loyalty, kindness, respectfulness, doing housework well and being 'born and raised in wedlock', according to a recommendation given for a teacher's wife. As many people died young, grandparents were in short supply. Usually at least one son went into the family business and entered the business (trade, peddling, craft) by helping out his father. Others sons helped out as well and some might move to another town upon marriage and open their operations or marry into a family with the same occupation and eventually take over the father-in-law's business. Jewish craftsmen were few and Jewish craft guilds did not have the rigid structure of Christian ones. Boys to be trained in a craft such as shoemaking or rope making might be trained by their father or if it was a new venture, sent off to a relative as an apprentice.

As detailed in the previous chapter, protected Jews paid a reception fee on being admitted to the town and annual protection taxes. In addition, individuals paid a tax on real estate purchases, an exit fee on their assets when they moved away, and fees to the government for burials, musicians who performed at marriage celebrations, and circumcisions. As with many towns and cities, non-resident Jews entering Uehlfeld had to pay a special toll, the *leibzoll*. Some communities also charged a fee for cattle herded through their gate. The Jewish community would pay taxes on community property like the cemetery and synagogue, and for special allowances such as the *eruv* (walkway) to the synagogue. Jewish communities often appointed one man to serve as a fiscal officer who handled community's payments and mediated disputes regarding tax payments. Although most taxes were paid in the local or regional currency, some might also be paid in goods such as chickens, sugar, peppers, and ginger. In addition to annual taxes, taxes might also be levied on the Jewish community to support local events such as the Easter and autumn fairs and to support particular institutions such as the regional prison or the support of orphans. Tax records suggest that there was considerable room for appeal and that officials were somewhat lenient, with the protection tax sometimes reduced or waived for widows, the financially distressed and the school teacher and the settlement tax halved for persons born in town who returned to live there later in life.

Laws governing Jewish rights to buy, own, sell and inherit real estate varied across Germany. In some regions Jews could own land, in others they could not; own several houses, in others just one; buy and sell property from and to Christians, in others property could only pass between Jews. In Uehlfeld, Jews who were encouraged to return to town after the Thirty Years' War in the second half of the seventeenth century were allowed to own property, both built property and land and to buy from and sell to Christians. Christian and Jewish Uehlfelders lived in four types of dwellings – estates, small estates, houses, and cottages. In the early eighteenth century and probably before then most Jews lived in cottages, typically one story of wood. Later most lived in stone or stucco multiple-story houses, which housed one, two, or even three families. Very few Jews owned an estate or small estate and those who did usually bought them for resale. One exception in the mid-1700s was a woman we know only as Reichel: 'Jewess Reichel has died, and her brother Jacob Weil in Furth has inherited the so-called Dietscher estate from her, valued 530 fl.' The year was 1765 and 530 fl. was a sizeable amount of money. Reichel had inherited the estate from her husband and then re-married with her new husband moving in with her, suggesting that she was indeed wealthy. Estates had, in addition to a large house, a barn, field, orchard and garden. The most valued possession in a house was the baking oven, afforded by only some families and rented out to others who lacked one. In addition to their dwellings, Jews in Uehlfeld were also allowed to own land, vineyards and ponds, and district records for the eighteenth century show occasional real estate transactions for these properties with Jews buying from and selling to one another and also from and to Germans. Because Jews did not farm, land was an investment, with the land typically sold off quickly.

The freedom Jews had to own property in Uehlfeld in the early 1700s was an exception, as rulers could and often did place restrictions on Jewish property ownership, often in an attempt to limit the size of Jewish communities. By the middle of the century, with Uehlfeld's Jewish community now firmly established, restrictions were enacted by the margrave. Following a practice common across Germany, Jews in Uehlfeld were still allowed to purchase property from Christians but had re-sell it to another Christian in a set time period, usually within a year or less. For example, in 1761 David Feist bought a house at auction in town but had to agree to sell it to a Christian within 'one-quarter year'. This was a new, restrictive change in policy from what had been in effect in the late seventeenth and early eighteenth centuries, when Jews in Uehlfeld could keep property purchased from Christians. Typical of these early real estate transactions was one in 1702:

> Real estate revenue due by Salomon and Schlanmel both Jews for a cottage which their father and father-in-law Low Jew 'der lange' had bought in their name in 1702 from Hanns Trescher who had bought it in 1699 from Jacob Franck and his wife, formerly Hanns Stiegler's widow, who had bought it in 1696 from Sir Johann Laubenter.

There is some satisfying irony in this transaction history as Johann Laubenter was the town's pastor who so vehemently resisted Jewish settlement in the late seventeenth and early eighteenth centuries. At that time, the margrave was encouraging Jewish settlement and making it easy to obtain a house or cottage made Uehlfeld more desirable. By mid-century the Jewish population was increasing, the pastor was complaining, and Jewish settlement needed to be contained. Nonetheless, those wanting to sell or buy property and keep it in Jewish ownership found ways around this restriction. One loophole allowed that property owned by a Jew before a Christian bought it could later return to Jewish ownership as with this purchase in 1763: 'The widow of Moises Pfeiffer in Kairlindach has purchased a field and a meadow from Johann Muhlberger who had bought them from Moises Pfeiffer.' Another way around the restriction was to purchase a property which no Christian would want: 'Moses Mannlein in Uehlfeld has bought the house of Johann Bart and was allowed to keep it because no other buyer could be found.' Third, and perhaps most commonly, more housing for newly-arriving Jews could be made available by sub-dividing an existing dwelling:

> Moses Aaron in Kairlindach has died without children. His widow has sold his half house, whose other half is owned by Viest Losar and which was taken out of the dismantled Kritzner estate, to the Jews Moses Gerst, Samuel Moses, and Juda Lasar, who were newly accepted. Viest Losar, the owner of the other half, had died and left a widow and four children under age. The widow has sold this half to Moses Gerst, Samuel Moyses, and Juda Lasar. The widow of Moses Aaron sold two fields. The widow of Viest Lasar inherited a field.

While the requirement to resell only to a Christian might limit Jewish settlement, it also created a new opportunity for those willing to take a risk and in modern parlance, 'flip' real estate. This is probably what David Feist was doing in 1761 when he bought the second house at auction, as he already owned a house he had inherited from his mother. Estates appealed to Jewish speculators who were allowed to purchase an estate and then divide it up into several properties and sell the pieces off for a profit to Christians and Jews. Speculators included both local men and others who came from cities. One of the most active speculators in Uehlfeld was Hayum Odensoss of Fürth who bought and sold much property in town in mid-century, one being the Zwanger estate in 1740:

> Zwanger (farming) estate in Uehlfeld was sold for 408 fl. To Hayum Odensoss and partners at the condition they resell it to a Christian within a year. He also bought an orchard for 20 fl., a field for 12 fl., and a basement and barn for 136 fl.

Later that year, 'Hayum Odensoss and partners sold the orchard for 43 fl', making a profit of 23 fl. and the remainder of the estate was sold off over the next few years.

Although we see variation across communities in property rights, there was less variation across small like Uehlfeld when it came to occupational structure, with Jewish men engaged in six major activities:

Religious specialists which might include the rabbi, assistant rabbi, cantor, *shochet*, school teacher and synagogue caretaker.

Craftsmen who made and sold products mainly to the Jewish community including butchers, tailors, rope makers, soap makers, and glass makers. Jewish craftsmen were few and were barred from the Christian craft guilds and often from selling to Christians and apprenticed only with other Jewish craftsmen.

Traders of farm products such as hops and wheat, cattle, cloth, wine, and leather usually produced by German farmers. Traders also lent money and extended credit with interest to suppliers and customers.

Peddlers of sundries, trinkets, used household items, and repurposed items.

Rag pickers who scavenged discarded textiles and repaired and resold them or fashioned new items such as curtains.

Beggars who solicited handouts of money, clothes, food and lodging from Jews and Christians and were the responsibility of the Jewish community.

Rural communities in addition to producing for their own use and sale in other communities, might also be called upon to supply farm and other products to the ruler whose court was in a city or large town. Thus, farm products from Uehlfeld flowed north to Bayreuth and Baiersdorf. Court Jews acted as the margrave's agent and bought from Jewish traders. In the 1750s Margrave Frederick of Ansbach and Bayreuth had his court in Bayreuth and his summer residence in Baiersdorf. He was hospitable to Jews, allowing them to re-settle in Bayreuth (they were exiled in 1515) and having a Jewish chess player and painter in his court. He also employed several court Jews, three of whom, Samson Heidenheimer and Wolff Hirsch, of Baiersdorf, who supplied his military with arms, and Moses Seckel of Bayreuth who ran his mint, bought large quantities of grain from Uehlfeld for the court in the 1750s. Like many court Jews, the men were supportive of the Jewish communities in their city and negotiated on the community's behaves with the margrave. Moses Seckel was instrumental in the Jewish re-settlement of Bayreuth, bringing twenty families there in the 1770s and purchasing a house from the margrave which he converted into a synagogue and residence.

Small-town Jewish communities did not have wealthy and influential court Jews like Moses Seckel, but Jews who traded expensive products such as leather, wine, and horses, land speculators and some craftsmen such as tanners were wealthier than others. Also wealthy were the occasional widows like Reichel mentioned above, who inherited a large house or small estate and some wealth from their husbands. Most widows had some property but no income, leading some to remarry and move away to join their new husband or relocate to live with their children, selling the property they inherited and taking the proceeds with them. Other remained in the community and with no income were supported by the community and often exempted from paying the protection tax. Wealthier families might own some land and had larger houses while poorer families lived in cottages or shared a house. For context it's important to remember that rural Jews did not form a distinct economic class, as most (from 60 to 80 per cent) of rural Germans were poor farmers into the nineteenth century and their lives insecure as well, not from fear of expulsion, but from crop failures and fluctuating market prices.

The lives of Christians like those of Jews were controlled to a significant extent by the laws and regulations made and enforced by the ruler and by the church and enforced by the pastor, priest, or bishop. But the rules governing their lives were less onerous, they were not a 'protected' people, paid less taxes, had more freedom of movement, had no limits on how many could live in a town, and most importantly, they enjoyed permanent residence.

In the typical town, Germans formed a hierarchy of thee socioeconomic classes. At the top were a few wealthy farmers who owned estates and might share ownership with the church or ruler, traveled by wagon or coach, and served as the town's officials (mayor, judge) and owned the local inn and/or tavern. Many towns also had a mill outside the village, with the miller also among the town's upper class. A second class was formed by the craftsmen or artisans, including the highly skilled (blacksmith, weaver, cooper, tailor, shoe maker, mason, carpenter), and the less-skilled (rope maker, tanner). The career path for a craftsmen and especially a highly skilled one was long and arduous: apprentice, journey man working in several different workshops, apprentice master with the guild, working in a guild workshop, finally one's own guild workshop. At the bottom were the 60 to 80 per cent of the residents who were famers, who owned or rented small holdings and could support themselves in good years but just as easily fall into poverty in bad ones. Many farmers earned additional income and more stability from work as low-level craftsmen. Finally, most towns had a few shops including usually a bakery and butcher shop although sometimes the Jewish butcher sold to both Jews and Christians.

Unlike the relationship with the noble, trade relationship between Jewish middle-men and the farmers was sealed by a handshake, not by written contract, and grounded in a mix of trust and distrust that came with years of negotiation (often over several generations) and the shared reality that each needed the other to survive. Jewish traders were also

7. The Uehlfeld market along the Haupstrasse in 1899. (Courtesy of Hans Gawronski)

money lenders, lending money to both the peasants they bought from and other Germans they sold to, with interest added to the unpaid balances. Sometimes they would lend money to the noble as well. The amount of principle and interest owed and demands that it be paid were a common source of conflict between Jews and Germans. The verbal agreements were also a source of mistrust, as peasants believed that they were instruments of Jewish exploitation. To control this alleged Jewish advantage, some rulers required that contracts be witnessed by a third party. The issue was so serious that in the 1770s in Middle Franconia a new regulation was instituted requiring a local official to review contracts between Jews and 'little people'. Thus, the primary relationship between Jews and Germans was an ongoing economic negotiation that might last for several generations over the price to be paid by Jews for products they purchased from Germans and the price to be paid by the other Germans who bought those products. At its core, it was a bargaining relationship with both parties often accusing the other of deception and fraud and disputes sometimes resolved by a beating administered by the German farmer to the Jewish trader.

Until the early 1800s, when the process of emancipation began to unfold, Jewish communities across Germany were more than just physical, social, and religious aggregations. Each was also a legal entity, which owned communal Jewish property, paid taxes, resolved disputes, and had representatives who negotiated on behalf of the community with the nobleman. Every localized Jewish settlement across Germany (there were over 1,000) was organized into one of these communities, each known as the *Jüdischen Gemeinde*. The entire Jewish population across all of Germany was lumped together as the *Israelitische Gemeinden*. In Bavaria after the Edict of Emancipation of 1813, the *gemeinden* no longer existed as legal entities but were now religious communities, which continued to serve much the same role as before in the Jewish communities and in German society. In some communities later in the century *gemeinde* re-established themselves as public corporations. The leader of the community was often the rabbi (if one was in residence) or a group of men who were selected because of their ability to negotiate on the community's behalf, and/or their economic savvy. In addition to leading the community in making decisions about community buildings and other matters, they served as the go-between with the nobleman and also settled disputes in the community.

As mentioned, disputes between Jewish traders and peddlers and their German customers were not uncommon. Disputes within the Jewish community were also not uncommon, typically involving property transactions, encroachments on one's trading territory, construction and maintenance of buildings, the hiring of the rabbi or other specialists, and negotiations with the nobleman and personal matters such as insults or adultery. Evidence in the form of *responsa* from German rabbis indicates that rabbis often did adjudicate family and community disputes in Jewish communities as well as advising on disputes with German neighbours and the rulers. But most disputes were handled within the community or by the margrave's managers or judges. The government handled disputes involving Jews and Germans if they were not settled between the disputants. Social control was maintained by judicial punishment (typically a fine but sometimes banishment) and the authorities took an active role in identifying and punishing those who broke its many rules and social and economic mores and even those who violated rules of the Jewish community. As regards the latter, the records show Jewish women and men being fined for buying meat out of town, thereby harming the Jewish butcher in town; unlawful slaughtering; indecent behaviour in the Jewish school; and unlawful selling of meat. That three of the four offenses involved the acquisition of meat points again to the centrality of *kashrut* in defining the Jewish community.

Germans frowned on adultery and premarital sex, and especially relations which produced illegitimate children, both among Jews and Christians. Those who were caught were named in town reports and punished, as with these two pairs:

> Pfeiffer Hirsch, son of Hirsch Nathan in Uehlfeld, was fined for fornication committed in Markt Schonfeld with Sara a Jewess from Lisberg and made her pregnant.
> Penalty for adultery between Lazarus Moises at Pahres and Elizabeth Neumayer a married woman. The penalty for adultery between said Elizabeth Neumayer and Lazarus Moises was reduced upon petition of his wife Meyle Pfeiffer.

Violent conflicts between Jews seem to have not been as common as non-violent economic crimes, although the lack of records makes this impossible to know. The mention of a gunfire in the Burghaslach synagogue, though, does give one pause. We know more about offences that came to the attention of German officials and are listed in the annual district reports, with one or two so noted every few years. Many others probably escaped official attention as they were undetected or not reported. Many of these were violent offences and what stands out is the variety of the combatants who went it with one another, as shown in this sample of entries from 1761 to 1783:

Brawl between brothers Low and Jacob Losar.
Brawl between Aaron Jacob of Pahres and Nochum Hess.
Brawl between the maidservant of Moses Jacob in Pahres and the wife of Salmon there.
Brawl between servant Jacob Abraham of Uehlfeld and Pfeieffer Isaac.
Brawl between David, son of Nochum Hess and Low Pfeiffer.
The following of Uehlfeld are fined for a brawl: The cantor, the prayer leader, Jacob Loesar, Moises Schlom, Maennlin Seeligmann, Lazarus Moses, Samuel Seckel. Victims were Lazarus Moses and Samuel Seckel.
Schoolmaster Israel Baer Moses is fined for odd behaviour against Lower Franken Rabbi Baruch David in Uehlfeld, and both are fined for a brawl.

This short list suggests that Jewish men and women might often – and certainly more than we have assumed – turn to physical violence to settle disputes between themselves. This may reflect a broader pattern of violent dispute settlement in rural German communities, as the German historian Stefanie Fischer notes that German farmers sometimes assaulted Jewish traders to settle disputes.

In addition to adultery, brawling and violations of Jewish rules, the authorities were much concerned with theft as Jewish peddlers and beggars were often accused of fraud or stealing items for their own use or for resale. Thus Jews were fined for all sorts of economic crimes: fraud, customs defraud, buying stolen sheep, stealing vegetables, stealing a pear, forging coins, buying a stolen tin, spending Sabbath in town without paying the entry fee and just plain stealing. And beyond these types of crimes, people were fined for a variety of other offences: remaining in town rather than emigrating, 'verbal injuries', 'verbal injuries' against the mayor, card playing, breaking a neighbour's windows, taking a widow as a lodger without notifying authorities and failure to present a substitute man for the guard. This last offence is intriguing as it reminds us that despite their outcaste status, Jews in the 1700s were still expected to perform some civic duties such as guarding the town gate.

Depending on the size of the community, each Jewish community supported various social, service and charitable groups, usually tied to the synagogue. Burghaslach, for example, over the years established a Talmud Torah Association, a Jewish Women's Association, a Burial Society, a chapter of the Association of Friends of Sabbath and a society to aid the poor, all which continued to operate into the 1930s, despite the decreasing Jewish population from the 1880s on.

The first society founded in a town and the most important was the Jewish Burial Society (*chevra kadisha*). All communities with a cemetery had one and those which didn't were served by the society in the town where the cemetery was located or by another society such as the Jewish Women's Society which would bury women who died without family. The ubiquity of burial societies reflected the reverence Judaism held for death and the strict ritual obligations of the family of the deceased and the community. With the high death rate in late medieval and early modern Europe, the societies were kept busy. Uehlfeld's Jewish community averaged about a half-dozen deaths a year, and people from other towns without their own cemetery also buried their dead in Uehlfeld. District records show, for example, the following burials in 1759:

> A son aged 8 days of Jewish beggar Abraham Jacob from Harburg on 27 Feb.
> A child aged 12 of a beggar Jew from Oettingen, on 8 Mar.
> A son of 14 days of Jacob Weil on 18 Apr. (all three died in Uehlfeld).
> Judlein a widow of Demantsfiirth died on 28 June.
> A daughter aged 3 of Marx Samuel at Uehlfeld.

Sometimes a burial society had both male and female members, other times men and women formed separate societies. Jewish law required treating the corpse with dignity; returning it to the earth quickly, adhering to ritual requirements for preparation of the body, a procession and prayer and providing compassion and support for the family during the mourning period. Members of the burial society were involved in each of these activities. In some communities, the society's mission might expand to include caring for the sick and preparing spiritually the terminally ill for death. Burial societies were equally responsible for burying those without families at hand, usually beggars and their children. Society members would become involved before death when possible, with a member present at death who would then transport the body to the mortuary (usually a small building within the cemetery), where it would be washed, shrouded and watched over until the funeral. Members of the society would then accompany the body to the grave as part of funeral procession, conduct the service and assist in filling the grave. Following the funeral, they would assist the family during the mourning period, bringing food and organizing and conducting the prayer services. The society also maintained the mortuary, the cemetery and the wall around them.

For at least 200 years and probably longer, Rindsbergs were part of this Uehlfeld Jewish community and as cattle dealers were part of the regional economic system. As we said, the first Rindsberg we know of was Feist Meier. We also know that he was married, although we don't know his wife's name. She died in 1786. They had four children whom we know of: Meier Feist (*c.* 1768 – Oct. 30, 1842), Josef (*c.* 1770 - before 1851), Theresa (*c.* 1771 – May 10, 1852), and David Feist (*c.* 1773/4 – Feb. 12, 1851). All four were born, lived, died and were buried in Uehlfeld. In 1768 Feist Meier paid the nobleman who ruled the town at the time a fee for the circumcision of his first son and presumably later, too, for his two younger sons, fees for circumcision being such a reliable source of income for the margrave that in the burial fee entries in the district's ledger it was noted if a male child died before circumcision. Presumably, if a boy died after circumcision, that fee needed to be collected as well as the burial fee. In 1793 Feist Meier owned two houses on what is now Raiffeisenstrasse, both used by his family. The two houses were near the synagogue and were likely the houses at 3 and 5 Raiffeisenstrasse owned one hundred years later by his grandsons David and Hirsch Rindsberg. Meier's three sons are especially significant figures in the Rindsberg family saga, since they were the first to take the Rindsberg surname and were the patriarchs of three lines of Rindsbergs who lived in Uehlfeld into the twentieth century and whose descendants live today in a half-dozen nations around the world. Daughter Theresa was genealogically significant also, marrying a man later known as Seligman Israel Dingfelder in Uehlfeld on 12 April 1796. The Dingfelders would become the town's leading Jewish family by the late nineteenth century and this early marriage created a bond between the Rindsbergs and Dingfelders that continued among those who survived the Holocaust and came to the United States.

As we've seen, the first Rindsberg ancestor we know of in Uehlfeld probably supported his family as a cattle dealer in the early 1700s. Cattle dealing then remained the occupation for some Rindsberg men for over two centuries, until the 1930s, when David and Julius Rindsberg's business was shut down by the Nazis. David Rindsberg ran his small operation from home, with cattle kept at night in the stone barn behind the house and chickens in a coop in front of the barn. During the day, cattle were grazed in his meadow a half-block away, just across the river. David would walk the five to ten head of cattle down the street, and across the wooden footbridge to the meadow. Sometimes he would enlist local youths to herd the cattle. One was Walter Reed, the grandson of his neighbour Hirsch Rindsberg, who visited in the summers. Eighty years later Walter could still recall as a boy lying in his bed at night dreaming about the cattle and reciting the names he had given them.

As already mentioned, most Jewish men like the Rindsberg cattle dealers were middle-men traders who sold the hops, grain, corn, animals

8. The former houses of two Rindsberg families in Uehlfeld in 1992. Rindsbergs lived in one or both of the houses at this location from the 1780s until 1938. (Courtesy of Walter Reed)

and products produced by the local peasants. Some others were peddlers who sold trinkets, sundries, and used household items door to door. Jewish traders also lent peasants money so that they could purchase seed, fertilizer and farm equipment in the spring before they had any income from their farms. Jew's central role in the agricultural economy didn't, however, change their status as social and religious and political outcastes. But, returning to their role as middle-men, it is important to remember that German Jews weren't and aren't unique among ethnic minorities in this regard. History and anthropology are rich with accounts of ethnic minorities that have filled this vital economic niche; examples include Asian Indians in East Africa, Chinese in Malaysia, and Korean greengrocers in New York.

In the United States today people sometimes stereotypically think of physician, attorney or Hollywood mogul as 'Jewish' occupations. In rural Germany cattle dealing was the Jewish occupation. From the 1600s into the first two decades of the twentieth century, more Jewish men were engaged in cattle dealing than in any other economic activity in rural Germany. In all farming areas of Germany, every town with a Jewish population had one or more Jewish cattle dealers and Jews had a virtual monopoly over the trade in many of those towns. As late as 1917, when many other occupations were now open to Jews, 60 per cent of cattle dealers in Germany were still Jewish. Cattle dealing, like other forms of Jewish peddling, was a family business – passed on from one generation to the next, usually from father to the oldest or youngest son.

Until the middle of the 1800s, nearly all cattle dealers operated on a small scale, usually working alone or with a son or two, buying from German farmers, and then selling to meat processors and tanners or other farmers. Weekly markets took place in many small towns with the Jewish dealers occupying the centre of activity in these social and economic gatherings. Jewish cattle dealers had long-standing relationships several generations deep with the German farmers and also with the meat and hide processors they sold to. These business relationships and the negotiations could be contentious, since farmers sometimes accused dealers of colluding to keep prices low and dealers accused farmers of selling them diseased or injured cattle. Each party tried to get the best price, engaging in the back and forth of ritualized bargaining, knowing that they had to reach a fair compromise so that both could make a profit and feed their families. Occasionally, true friendships developed between the dealers and farmers.

Each cattle dealer worked a set territory (*medine* in Yiddish) and informal agreements (again, passed from generation to generation) among the dealers ensured that each dealer had exclusive rights to his territory.

Traders of other farm products had like arrangements and incursions into another trader's *medine* was a common source of conflict in Jewish communities. The peasants were paid in cash, and the dealers sold on credit to the butchers and processors, adding interest to the unpaid balance. In addition, in tough times they would lend peasants money and even rent them a cow for its milk. Negotiations were conducted in Yiddish or some combination of Yiddish and German, and even after Yiddish faded from Jewish homes in the early 1800s, trading was still often conducted in a Yiddish-German trade language which provided a specialized and familiar trade lexicon for the participants. To aid communication, translation guides were published, such as one in Neustadt entitled *Some Phrases in the Jewish Language of Business,* which provided Yiddish and German versions of useful phrases such as:

> It's too cheap.
> She is old.
> The ox is too big.
> The horse is deaf.
> The calf is sick.
> The scale is off.
> It has a good coat.
> Now he is penniless.

Depending on the condition of the cattle and market demand, the cattle might be taken directly to market or sold to another farmer or kept by the dealer for a period of time. Dealers had barns where they kept cattle at night and usually a small meadow where they grazed them during the day.

Cattle dealing could be hard work with long hours. The dealer would frequently leave home on Sunday, travelling by foot or wagon, with his week's supply of kosher meat, bread and fruit. He'd travel across his *medine*, buying and selling at town and regional markets. Nights were spent in Jewish inns or German inns that catered to Jewish travellers or with Jewish families. The trader would return home on Friday and attend service in the synagogue and rest on the Sabbath. Sunday he'd be off again. David Rindsberg's territory was evidently not large and much of his trading was done in town and in neighbouring communities.

It was no coincidence that the three Jewish brothers in Uehlfeld who first took the name Rindsberg were two cattle dealers and a butcher and that the Sturm kin in Burghaslach included tanners, leather dealers and cattle dealers. Cattle dealers supplied the raw material for butchering and tanning, and it was financially wise to keep the activities in the same family. Some cattle dealers also doubled as butchers, keeping the entire operation to themselves. Because Jewish dietary laws prohibited the eating of certain cuts of meat and internal organs, Jewish butchers sold these parts to non-Jews. A number of cattle dealers sold horses as well, and some specialized exclusively in horse dealing. Horse dealing required more capital than cattle dealing and was considered a higher-status occupation. Jewish dietary law kept Jews from selling swine.

The number of cattle dealers was rivalled by the number of Jewish hops dealers, with many also trading other farm products such as wheat or corn. As with cattle dealers, many towns had more than one hops dealer. The hops industry, from farm to stein, was driven by the demand for beer, Germany's national beverage and the liquid symbol of its national identity. In Bavaria, where beer was perhaps most popular, the Bavarian *Reinheitsgebot* (German Beer Purity Law) first set forth in 1516 established the hops industry by limiting the components of beer to barley, hops and water and made demand high for Bavarian hops throughout Germany.

Rural Jews were also much involved in the textile market, but unlike in Eastern Europe and later in the United States, in Germany in the 1700s they were almost exclusively sellers, not producers. The German guilds blocked entrance by Jews and strongly supported laws which prohibited Jews from making and selling new clothing, the most lucrative sector of the industry. Thus Jewish traders and peddlers sold items such as curtains or unfinished fabric and repaired clothing while rag pickers repaired and repurposed and then sold discarded cloth products. As with cattle and hops dealing, Jewish participation in the garment trade was transformed in the nineteenth century with Jews becoming major players as tailors and factory and store owners who employed German workers, who made and sold all sorts of textile products – coats, hats, caps, undergarments, clothing and umbrellas.

The Jewish occupational structure in Uehlfeld in the early 1800s, as the emancipation era began to unfold, was typical of farm towns: ten hops traders with several of them also selling other farm products and dry goods; seven cattle dealers and other men who sold spices, draperies, soft goods, hardware, wool, hides and leather, glass, furs, wine, tobacco, flour, iron and needlework. Except for one man who ran a shop in town, they were all traders whose customers were mainly outside town. Jewish craftsmen in town were limited to a shoemaker, rope maker, soap maker, baker and butcher. The Jewish occupations were rounded out by the religious specialists – the rabbi, cantor, school caretaker, school teacher and kosher butcher/*shochet*, although only the rabbi and teacher were full-time positions.

The small-town Jewish life described in this and the previous chapter began to change in the late 1700s as the emancipation process emerged first in the north and later in the south. In Bavaria the year 1813 was especially significant with the enactment of the Edict of Emancipation, marking the official beginning of the emancipation process that eventually led to freedom and citizenship. We now turn to this process and its broadening transformation of the Jewish German experience.

6

Emancipation and Transformation

In 1993, Erwin Kahn, a man from the small farming community of Nineveh in upstate New York, sent my mother a large manilla envelope. It bulged with copies of Uehlfeld town records and documents from the 1800s and early 1900s with details about the town's Jewish residents and the community. Erwin was a Dingfelder descendant (his mother Martha came to the United States in the 1920s) and he had spent several vacations from his teaching position in Spain in Uehlfeld gathering genealogical information about his Dingfelder ancestors and also the Rindsbergs, because of the close ties between the two families. One of the documents he generously included was a copy of the town's several-page-long Jewish Register or *Matrikel* for 1818, a hand-written spreadsheet neatly listing the Jewish male residents of town, the surnames they had just taken for themselves and the names of their children. I ran my eyes down the second page, and there it was, *Rindsberg*! Not just one, but three Rindsbergs – listed as Rindsberg I, Rindsberg II and Rindsberg III. It was an especially exciting genealogical moment, as I am named David after David Rindsberg, the grandson of the David Feist who, with the authority of that register, became David Feist Rindsberg or Rindsberg III. In 1818 all Jewish men in town took surnames for the first time, one step in the emancipation process that was already underway in Prussia and Austria and other states and would continue to sort itself out over the next fifty or so years. Patriarch Feist Meier's three sons were now Meier Feist Rindsberg, Josef Rindsberg and David Feist Rindsberg. We believe that the three brothers took the name Rindsberg because it was based on their occupation. Rindsberg translates as 'cattle on the hill', and two of the brothers were cattle dealers and the third a butcher and possibly a cattle dealer as well. The name suggests that kept the cattle they were readying for market on a hillside pasture. We don't know if it is the same pasture, but the name Rindsberg still fit David and Julius Rindsberg in 1938. Their meadow was a gently sloping rise just across the river from their home.

The Rindsberg brothers and other men in town took surnames in 1818 because the 1813 Bavarian Edict of Emancipation required Jews to take surnames. The history of family names is a fascinating topic, but in Germany it is also complicated, both for Germans and Jews. It is worth noting that not

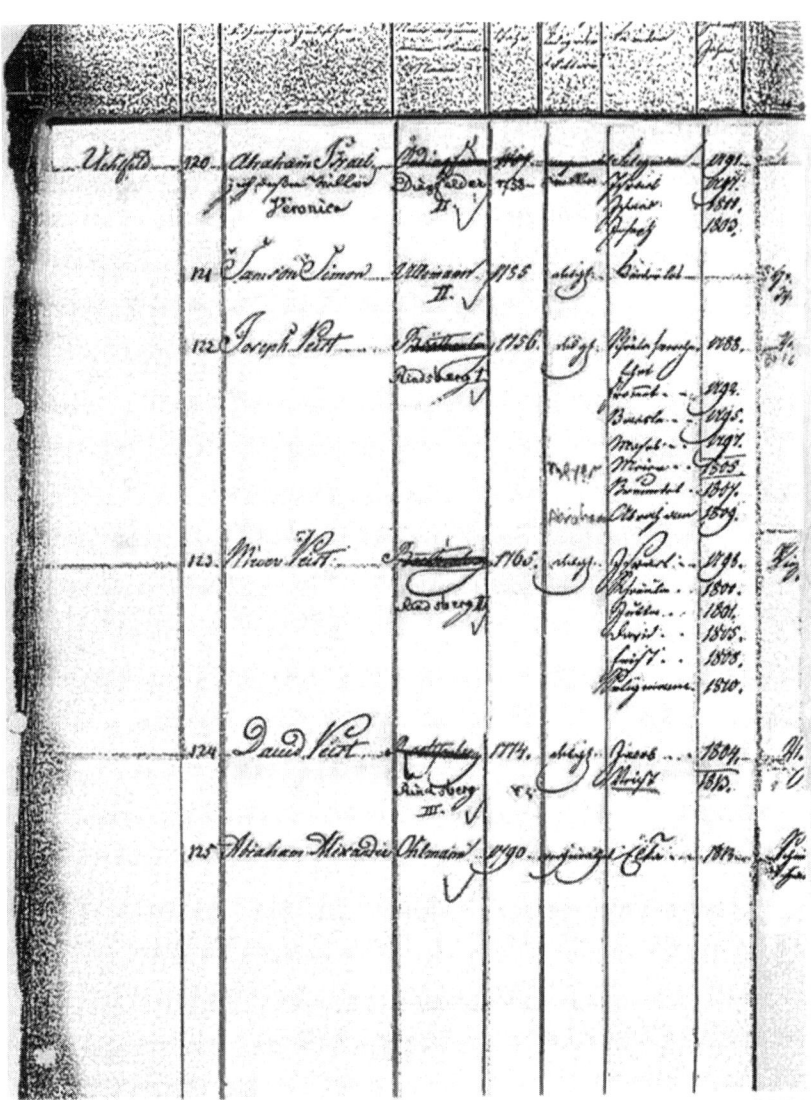

9. A page from the census of the Uehlfeld Jewish community in 1818, listing the householders, their new surnames and their children's names.

only Jews but also many Germans did not have surnames until fairly recently, with many rural Germans not taking them until the eighteenth century. The first Jews to take surnames were a few religious scholars who took their surnames in the fifteenth century or even earlier. Over the next few centuries, some other men also took surnames; they were mostly wealthy men in cities such as Frankfurt and Hamburg. Some men chose their surnames based on where they lived or some feature of their house while others retained the surnames they brought with them when they immigrated to Germany from Austria and Portugal. These early surnames were not necessarily permanent, as they might change when a man moved to a new house or community. In Bavaria most Jews at the opening of the nineteenth century were still identified only by their given names. A few years later when required to take surnames, most were free to choose their surnames, although government officials had to approve them. In some other regions people had less freedom as officials assigned Jews surnames that identified them as Jewish. Many rural Jews in Bavaria took names based on their given name by adding an ending like 'stein' or 'berg', or their occupation or a physical feature of the landscape. Since several Jewish men in a town often had the same occupation, often as cattle dealers or hops dealers, some creativity was needed in selecting unique names. The Tuchman family recalled that their ancestor, Marx Tuchman, had to do just that in 1818:

> When my grandfather was asked by the district judge in Neustadt what German name he would accept, he was keen to get some sort of short name and suggested, in view of the fact that he was a hops trader, the name Hopf (hops), but this was refused him as someone else (Simon Hopf) had previously adopted this name. Since my grandfather also traded in hop-cloth (Höpfentuch; hop-sacking), he came up with the idea of accepting the name Tuchmann (cloth-man).

The 1818 Uehlfeld register lists the first surnames as: Aischberg, Erlich, Dingfelder, Engländer, Eosenthal, Flosman, Goldberg, Gutherz, Heidenheimer, Hopf, Kohn, Läutershäuser, Lehmann, Lewino, Mandelbaum, Rindsberg, Rosenfeld, Sachs, Schwab, Tuchman, Ullman, Wallfisch and Wasserman.

One thrill of doing genealogy is finding oddities in one's family history which makes one's family unique. One oddity of the Rindsberg genealogy is that Feist Meier's three sons in Uehlfeld were evidently the only men who took the Rindsberg name in all of Germany. The late Walter Reed (born in Lower Franconia as Werner Rindsberg in 1924) of Wilmette, Illinois, who conducted extensive research on the Rindsberg genealogy, tells us that every Rindsberg descendant he identified – in Germany, the U.S., England, South Africa, Israel and Argentina – is descended from Feist Meier and his three sons. Reed's discovery is supported by Valerie Johnson of Cincinnati, Ohio (another Rindsberg descendant) who compiled a genealogy of several hundred Rindsberg descendants in the United States from the mid-1800s until about 1990, and traced each one back to Feist Meier.

Taking surnames was but one element of the emancipation process which played out over the first seventy or so years of the nineteenth century across the German states. Emancipation progressed at different speeds in different regions and moved more slowly in Bavaria than in Prussia and Austria. Jewish emancipation did not develop in political and economic isolation but, rather, took place in the context of and was influenced by several other major transformations during this especially tumultuous century in German history. These include periods of political instability related to the consolidation of the German states and the emergence of new forms of government, failure (the Revolution of 1848) and finally success at political unification (1868-71), politically-motivated violence, industrialization, large-scale emigration from small towns to cities and America and periods of economic expansion and contraction.

Within this broad sweep of events, the emancipation of Jews in Germany proved to be a transformation in role and status of enormous significance in German and Jewish history, a development that took on special importance when the German Jewish community was eradicated in the Holocaust only seventy years later. The temporal sequence of emancipation followed by some sixty years of freedom and assimilation and then the Nazi and Holocaust period has led historians, political scientists and others to study and speculate about possible causal links between the first two periods and the third. They wonder: did the freedom and success Jews gained from emancipation in some way cause a revival of a particularly virulent form of anti-Semitism leading to the Holocaust? This question remains unanswered to everyone's satisfaction even though, or perhaps because, unlike earlier periods in Jewish German history, we actually do know a great deal about Jewish emancipation and the resulting changes in the Jewish experience. In addition, several other basic questions remain under debate: when did the emancipation process begin, why did it begin, what was its goal, did it harm or help the Jewish German population? All of these questions remained unanswered to everyone's satisfaction and open to interpretation and some of the details which follow about the emancipation process in southern Germany do touch on these and other questions, but my intent here is not to enter these debates.

What is not subject to much debate is that the philosophical and political basis for Jewish emancipation in Germany was the broader move toward freedom and equality for all across Western Europe which began in the eighteenth century with the major transformations tied to the Enlightenment, the formation of European nation-states and the French Revolution, which gave Jews French citizenship. An important influence on

Germany's move toward emancipation came in 1780, when Hapsburg Emperor Joseph II, the ruler of Austria, Hungary, and Bohemia and Moravia, opened ghettos, abolished the Jewish badge (yellow patch of cloth) and allowed Jews to enter all occupations and public schools and universities.

In Bavaria, a key early push toward Jewish emancipation came through Bavaria's alignment with France during the Napoleonic Wars (1803-1815), leading to the incorporation of Franconia and neighbouring regions into Bavaria between 1803 and 1817. The incorporation of Franconia (actually just eastern Franconia) into Bavaria increased Bavaria's Jewish population ten-fold. After several centuries of massacres and expulsions, Bavaria's Jewish residents had nearly all fled by about 1551 and Jews did not return and then only in small numbers until nearly a century and half later. By 1800, Bavaria had only about 3,000 Jewish residents and most towns and cities had no Jewish residents at all. Franconia, though far smaller than Bavaria, had 30,000 Jewish residents who formed about 2 per cent of its population. Thus, with Franconia added to the kingdom, Bavaria now had a substantial Jewish population and the state again faced the question faced in other regions – what to do about its Jews or, what was already being phrased across Western Europe as the 'The Jewish Question'. The options Bavaria had exercised earlier, expel those who lived there and deny settlement to others, was no longer an option in the early 1800s political environment.

Napoleon was hardly a supporter of Jewish emancipation but he gave Jews in Germany limited civil rights, opened ghettos and initiated policies and laws that stirred the process that finally led to Jewish legal equality by 1871. But Napoleon's reforms were only temporary, with some quickly removed from the books by various German state governments including Prussia and Bavaria, soon after his defeat at Waterloo in 1815. They were just an opening effort, and in Bavaria as elsewhere in Germany progress toward emancipation then played out over a period of some sixty years. The process was hardly smooth with rights granted and rescinded several times and instituted on different schedules across Germany and even across different cities and towns in the same region. In Bavaria, emancipation policy was set by Bavaria's king, but district and local officials had considerable leeway in how and when the policies were enforced and some would drag their bureaucratic feet while others pushed forward. The year 1871 (or 1868 in the north) is typically cited as the year of emancipation, although it is important to remember that some rights such as economic ones or even full citizenship were actually granted earlier in some cities and regions; for example, in Prussia in 1850, Nuremburg in 1861, and Frankfurt in 1864.

The early steps toward emancipation took place in the context of broad and deep and sometimes unsettling government reforms across Germany.

In 1806 Bavaria became the Kingdom of Bavaria and in 1818 a constitutional monarchy. The Kingdom was ruled by a king and his ministers and managed by regional, district and city and town administrators. The newly-formed parliament with limited powers was composed of an appointed upper chamber representing the aristocracy and nobility and an elected (with limited suffrage) lower house representing the people and towns. This new government structure proved itself enormously important to Jewish emancipation as it was decisions made by the king, his ministers and the parliament which propelled emancipation forward, delayed it or pulled it back.

But the kingdom's Jewish population, living mainly in Franconia, was left out of the new political structure. It had no representation in parliament although it was guaranteed religious freedom. The role of Jewish communities and individuals in Bavarian society had already been defined in the 'The Edict of June 10, 1813 Regarding the Status of Persons of Jewish Faith in the Kingdom of Bavaria', commonly referred to as the less wordy and more manageable *Judenedikt*, Emancipation Edict, Jew Edict, or Matriculation Law. The thirty-four articles of the Edict gave Jews religious freedom, citizenship, and more legal rights and economic opportunity than they had enjoyed previously. But the rules and procedures in the Edict hardly prescribed a straight path to full rights and emancipation and was actually more restrictive than similar edicts in other regions including Austria and Prussia. It was meant to bring the Jewish community into Bavarian society while limiting Jewish influence. Jewish men were required to pledge allegiance to Bavaria, prove that they had permission to live in their towns, take a surname, and serve in the military. Jewish influence was restricted by limiting the number of Jewish families permitted to live in Bavarian cities and towns. Jews were allowed to remain in communities where they already lived but could not settle in communities which had no Jews at the time. At the time Edict was issued, Uehlfeld was one of seventeen towns and one city (Bayreuth) in the Bayreuth district. Uehlfeld with a population of thirty-seven Jewish families had the second-largest Jewish population of the towns. To remain in their own town or city, Jewish men and sometimes women (typically a widow) had to obtain official permission – to be placed on the *matrikel* or *Juden matrikel* – which required the head of the household to show that he had an occupation and could support his family. This meant that the heads of the households of the 2,711 Jews living in seventy-four communities in Middle Franconia had to submit to the humiliating registration process, in which they had to show the district official evidence of residence and occupation and swear allegiance to Bavaria. The Uehlfeld register for 1818 mentioned above records that the three Rindsberg brothers already had that evidence on file - Joseph since 1786, Meier since 1796, and David since 1810 in the regional offices in Neustadt and Dachsbach. When the administrative process was competed for the entire town, thirty-three men and four women (all widows of formerly protected Jewish men) were listed as having community rights and seven other men were listed as owning houses in town but not having rights, although they were allowed to remain.

With the Edict falling far short of giving Jews full rights and equality, some Jewish leaders kept pushing forward, taking advantage of the new political structure which allowed citizens to bring their grievances and wishes to the lower house parliament. One who took the lead in Bavaria was Rabbi Samson Wolf Rosenfeld, rabbi of the Uehlfeld rabbinate since 1808. Rosenfeld was something of a Renaissance man with interests, passions and abilities exceeding those of most other Bavarian rabbis. For Rosenfeld, rights also included a public education and a greater role for women in society and toward those ends he taught in the Uehlfeld Jewish school (unusual for a rabbi at the time) and instituted religious confirmation for girls at age twelve. A prolific author, Rosenfeld also tried his hand at publishing, issuing in 1835 and 1836 the periodical *Das Füllhorn: ein zeitblatt zunaechst fuer und ueber Israeltin,* a vehicle for publishing political tracts aimed at the Jewish community as well as poetry, including some by the female poet Henriette Ottenheimer.

He was a rabbi in the last generation of pre-modern German rabbis and a moderate religious reformer (discussed below), with his religious reforms linked with his fight for Jewish rights, forcefully expressed in sermons, pamphlets, and petitions to the Bavarian parliament. He was a strong proponent of Jews moving from traditional Jewish to 'German' occupations and he encouraged men to abandon peddling for farming, shop-keeping and crafts.

In 1819 Rosenfeld authored a lengthy petition entitled 'Appeal for Equality for Jews in Bavaria' and led a group of Bavarian rabbis in presenting it to the newly-formed lower house in Munich. In addition to a general appeal for equal rights, the petition argued especially for more economic opportunity for Jews so they could move from peddling to the trades and professions. Hearing complaints of resistance in the form of bureaucratic delays in the rural craft guilds, Rosenfeld suggested that trade schools be established in cities and Jewish men be allowed to live and work there. Rosenfeld and his contingent were optimistic that their petition would be getting a fair hearing, as some liberal-leaning reformers in the lower house had indicated support as they sensed growing support for their liberal reforms.

Unfortunately, the wish for liberal reforms and greater rights for Jews was not shared by all of Bavaria's nor all of Germany's citizens and the hope that Rosenfeld's petition and other rights initiatives elsewhere in Germany would be accepted and turned into law was quickly crushed when a minority but loudly anti-Jewish slice of the Franconian population violently objected. Their displeasure quickly turned violent in the so-called Hep! Hep! riots which broke out in Würzberg in 1819 and then spread across Franconia, much of Germany and into Poland and Denmark. As in the past, Jews were assaulted and some killed and their businesses and homes ransacked in a brutal statement of opposition to Jewish equality. Many local governments acted to quell the riots but often did too little, too late. The physical damage was slight compared to assaults of the past; the lasting damage was to the 1819 equality initiative in particular and the push for Jewish rights in general. The Bavarian and other parliaments heard their loudest and most violent constituents and backed off from considering Jewish rights. Rosenfeld's petition was formally rejected in 1922, the Bavarian parliament noting that the time was not right.

The origin of the cry Hep! Hep!, shouted by the rioters as they attacked Jews and their property, is unclear. It most likely was a re-purposing of the call used by sheep-herders to now 'herd' Jews. The riots were apparently set off by the petitions submitted by Rosenfeld and others for a grant of immediate equal rights for Jews. Viewed from the perspective of the German farmer or small businessman, the timing was not likely to win their support or even their indifference. They were suffering and facing an uncertain future. The harsh summer of 1816 produced widespread famine and poverty and many farmers and small businessmen owed large sums to Jewish traders and moneylenders. In addition, Germans were anxious about and still finding their way in the new German political structure, now composed of just 39 states (down from over 300 polities) in the loose German Confederation, created by the Congress of Vienna in 1814 and 1815 to replace the Holy Roman Empire. The old principalities, duchies, margraviates, etc. were gone and new forms of government such as the constitutional monarchy in Bavaria were being organized and beginning to function. It was not an atmosphere in which reforms seen as benefiting the Jewish minority would be accepted, let alone supported, by the nervous majority.

Nonetheless, Jewish reformers (many of whom like Rosenfeld were also Reform Judaism reformers), and their liberal German supporters kept up the fight for relief from the more restrictive requirements of the Edict or for total equality, although they failed to achieve any legislative relief in 1831, 1834, 1845, and 1847. This continuing drive for Jewish rights paralleled and in some ways meshed with the much broader effort across the German states for liberal government reforms including broader suffrage, worker rights, an end to monarchial rule, and unification of the thirty-nine states into a single German nation. Leading the reform movement were intellectuals, liberals, the middle class and workers. Their efforts culminated in the Revolution of 1948 playing out in riots, assaults (sometimes on Jews and their property), and protests in several states including Bavaria and Prussia and three conferences bringing all the interest groups together to try and forge national unity and institute democratic reforms. Neither the violence nor the conferences produced the desired reforms, as the revolution collapsed in the face of competing interests between the middle class and the workers and between the states as well as the political inexperience of many of the reformers. When it was all over in 1850 the aristocracy and monarchs were still in control and many of the liberal leaders fled Germany for the United States.

The German Revolution of 1848 was the German version of the European Revolutions of 1848. The revolutions began in Sicily and then spread to France, Germany, Italy and the Austrian Empire and influenced

10. Problems of the Day. This lithograph and text from 1847-48 show a conversation between a Jewish peddler, who wears an Iron Cross and a lower class German friend, who sympathetically questions him about his lack of rights, as a Jew, despite being a decorated veteran. This understanding of the Jewish situation was typical of pre-1848 liberalism. (Courtesy of the Leo Baeck Institute, New York)

politics in other nations as well. As in Germany, the revolutions were led by liberals who sought to end monarchial rule and institute democratic reforms. The movement was meant to be peaceful, but insurrections and riots broke out in France, Germany and Austria. As in Germany, the revolutions produced little immediate change, finding some success only in France.

The Revolution of 1848 doomed the new legislation offered in 1847 granting Jews full rights in Bavaria. Thus, many were surprised when in May 1849 the lower house took up a new bill to grant Jews full rights. The legislation ultimately failed after initial success, but the process by which it failed highlights the continuing strong opposition to Jewish rights still expressed loudly and very publicly in the mid-nineteenth century. Emancipation was supported by Protestants, merchants and Bavarian government officials and opposed by Catholics, farmers, artisans, mayors and the aristocracy. Getting behind the initiative were several key ministers who apparently had the silent approval of King Maximilian II. Reflecting the liberal shift in the lower house, the new law granting Jews full rights passed by a vote of ninety-one to forty in December, with strongest support coming from the representatives of the Protestant provinces and the strongest opposition from the Catholic ones. But, the citizenry were hardly as supportive and accounts in the press of the lower house's deliberations and vote spurred many citizens into action. In the two months following the vote, Bavarian citizens and community officials sent 1,751 petitions to the legislature, with only six supporting the legislation. Although many petitions voiced local concerns, several common objections to Jewish equality appear across the petitions, as in the following one from the town of Hilders, signed by eighty-three residents, the mayor, treasurer, town council and parish priest:

> More than any other region, the people of Lower Franconia surely had the most legitimate reason to expect, instead of having the Hebrews granted 'greater', indeed completely 'equal' rights, exactly the 'opposite', namely energetic protection against the excessive abuses that these people have already notoriously made of the rights granted to them 'earlier'. We expect protection and more effective laws against Jewish swindling, against their fraud and usury, against the systematic exploitation of townspeople and countrymen, who, quite commonly, after an initially small debt to the Jews, soon find themselves so ensnared that they can longer avoid ruin. But, instead of such expected protection 'against' Jews, the Christian people are, conversely, to be totally delivered to Jewish oppression and exploitation through the grant of completely equal rights to the nation. After so many families

have been reduced to beggary by them, so many bloody tears extracted because of them, we are to see them henceforth even as our 'judges', are to open to them all 'ministerial' and 'government offices', are to all Jewish 'rent officials' to harass the people and to play into the hands of their fellow tribesmen, and 'we', the Christians, are to bow before their ilk! They are to be allowed to meddle in all of our communal affairs, indeed even have a say in our Church and endowment matters! Such rights are granted to an alien people that is hostile to Christians everywhere, that to this day harbours the same hate toward our religion with which it once nailed the Saviour to the Cross. (Harris, 1994: 252)

Mirroring the vote in parliament, opposition was strongest in the Catholic provinces, which had the fewest Jewish residents, a common occurrence in ethnic relations in many nations, in which majority peoples with little personal knowledge of minority peoples typically develop negative stereotypes of the minority. Reading the mood of their constituents, the upper house again rejected the legislation, delaying full equality in Bavaria until the unification of Germany in 1871, although some communities such as Nuremberg granted it earlier.

While political reforms leading to equality were moving slowly in the states, the integration of Jews into the German economy was moving along more rapidly, with especially rapid economic integration leading some cities such as Nuremberg and Frankfurt to grant Jews full rights before full citizenship was granted at the state or national level. Economic transformation in Bavaria began with the Edict's desire to change 'Jewish' occupations, and especially peddling which the Hilders townsfolk had so vehemently objected to:

> To divert the Jews from their traditional insufficient and antisocial forms of occupation, and to open to them every permitted source of income compatible with their current status, they shall have access to all common civil occupations such as agriculture, skilled trades, the running of factories and manufactures, and generally recognized forms of commerce under the following regulations; by contrast, the currently prevailing peddler's trade is to be phased out gradually, but as expeditiously as possible. (Bavarian Edict of Emancipation, 1813)

The Uehlfeld town register for the years 1819 and 1820 provides a snapshot of Jewish economic activity in town and across much of Germany as the emancipation process began to unfold. In those years, Jewish men were still engaged mainly in traditional rural Jewish occupations. The largest number – fifteen – were in textiles. One manufactured calico cloth and the others traded drapery, curtains, ribbon and other cloth goods. Most others were also traders – twelve traded cattle, seven dealt hops, three traded household goods and one each cereals, iron and leather. Three men ran shops in town. The religious vitality of the community which served as the district rabbinate was evident in the presence of a resident rabbi, two *shochetim*, the school teacher, and the school assistant. Jewish communities supported those unable to work or with limited income; in Uehlfeld it was a retired *shochet* and a teacher and two men who were too ill to work.

The Edict soon had its intended effect on Jewish occupations. Men began moving out of peddling and into farming and the crafts and traders began expanding their businesses or opening shops. In 1825, Rabbi Rosenfeld, commented on the community's economic progress in his letter of application for the rabbi's position in Bamberg:

> Certainly worth mentioning is the local Israelite's increased level of industrial, commercial and civic activity. Thus, already five Jewish craftsmen are based here and several others seek to achieve this goal as well. The greater part participates in solid, middle-class trade and agriculture and several have taken effective measures to leave their plots in better shape than in the past. So my ambition to convey to my co-religionists the goals of the state and of civilization has met the most beautiful successes. (Allemania-Judaica-Uehlfeld)

It didn't happen immediately, but over the next few decades and especially after 1850 Jewish men and some women dramatically altered their economic profile – traders became shop keepers and distributors, local cattle dealers became regional and even international ones, hops dealers moved to cities and become brokers and speculators, and garment traders opened factories and shops, and some moved into or expanded the more lucrative, fur, leather, and wine trades. A few bought up land and farmed and a few others became craftsmen, but relatively few chose these occupations which put them into direct competition with Germans. For the most part, Jews built on their commercial knowledge, skills, experience, and networks. Details on how these occupational changes transformed several families and altered the Jewish class system later in the century are discussed in the following chapter.

Education had been always important to Jewish parents but it had been mainly religious education and on-the-job occupational training until the later 1700s when interest grew, especially in cities, in providing public education for Jewish boys and girls. That became possible for all, not just the wealthy who could hire private tutors, in 1804 when the Bavarian authorities required Jewish children to receive a public education, followed by the Edict of Emancipation which allowed Jewish communities to provide public education in their religious schools as an alternative to their children attending the Christian schools for public education. As we have seen over and over, German government agencies were highly structured and bureaucratic, regularly issuing numerous rules and regulations concerning all aspects of life. In the 1820s the Bavarian authorities began raising and standardizing teacher qualifications, as they had also done for rabbis, and also codifying building and classroom construction. Many Jewish communities could not meet these standards as few of their religion teachers had the requisite education or experience and many schools were the old religious schools – usually a room or two in the teacher's house. And even if they could find a qualified teacher, many communities did not have the funds to pay him, because they were too small or because they had too many poor to support (some communities were supporting about twenty percent of their members in the early 1800s). Uehlfeld was an exception as it already had an acceptable school building, the old synagogue having been converted into a school in 1818 and it had also had long employed a teacher and sometimes an assistant. Plus, its rabbi, Samson Wolf Rosenfeld, was literate and fluent in German and taught in the school.

The experience of Lichtenau, another Middle Franconian town with a Jewish population comparable to that of Uehlfeld, provides some insight into the hurdles facing many communities trying to meet the new Bavarian standards. Lichtenau's problems began in 1821 when the government, as elsewhere in Germany, ordered that all 'foreign' teachers be dismissed. Foreign usually meant Polish, as many Jewish teachers in Germany had emigrated there from Poland. The Lichtenau Jewish community then needed to replace the departed teacher, preferably with a man who could teach both the religious and public curriculum. They soon ran up against the new Bavarian regulation requiring teachers to have university training and/or experience that enabled them to teach the elementary school curriculum in German. School books and also books used in Jewish religious education were to be in German.

The applicant they selected was Simon Rosenthal, a teacher, cantor and butcher who had been a protected resident with his wife Maria and a daughter in Menzingen, a town in Baden-Württemberg. By Jewish community standards, his resume was impressive – eleven years' teaching experience, with both he and Maria coming with sterling recommendations from a town official in Menzingen and also from the leader of the Jewish community of Bischhoschein, where he had taught before then. He was lauded as peaceful, diligent, honest, loyal, kind and respectful. Maria shared those same superlatives and also 'refrained from slander', 'did her housework well', and was 'born and raised in wedlock', giving us some insight into the behaviours considered desirable and undesirable by the Bavarian authorities. It also didn't hurt that Rosenthal was from Franconia, having been born and raised in Uehlfeld. His application and supporting documents was then sent up to the district office, then up to the provincial office, and then over to the Supreme Jewish Council in Baden who had the final say. The Council was careful, adhering to the Bavarian guidelines for teachers:

> January 20, 1822. The Baden Supreme Jewish Council has no objection to the hiring of Simon Rosenthal from Menzingen as a butcher and teacher. If he has not passed a teacher's exam, the Jewish children must also attend the German school.
>
> The county office writes to the Jewish district council at Bischofsheim: Simon Rosenthal must pass an examination of his ability to teach or offer proof that he has passed such an exam; otherwise the Jewish children must attend the German school at Lichtenau.
>
> Feb. 11, 1822. Burgermeister Dietrich writes to the district court that Rosenthal was asked about his ability to teach non-religious elementary subjects and he declared that he cannot prove that he can. The Jewish children are required to attend the German school.

The community followed the council and the burgermeister's orders; Rosenthal was hired, the children went for their public education to the Christian school. It worked out well. Rosenthal taught the religious school for 40 years and also served at times as a butcher, cantor, prayer leader and *shochet*. He and Maria added six additional children to the town's population.

In 1843 Rosenthal and the Lichtenau Jewish community faced a new educational problem – how to bring Rosenthal's Jewish school up to Bavarian standards:

> May 3, 1843. The annual report of the physician's inspection of the Jewish school is presented. The district office in Rheinbischofsheim must take care to correct the missing and deficient conditions of the Jewish school house in Lichtenau.
>
> May 15, 1843. The district office writes to the synagogue council in Lichtenau that the school room is not actually 7 feet high and the windows are only 2.5 feet high and would not let enough light in, and it is facing south and would be extremely hot in the summer and cold

in the winter. The synagogue council must submit plans to correct these deficiencies.

The synagogue council reports that the school room is not equipped as required by law, but it is only used by 10 to 12 children at one time, for whom there is sufficient space, and no smells were found therein. The teacher was also satisfied with the room and never became ill there and neither did the students.

Due to the many poor that need to be supported, we are presently unable to afford any expenses for this, especially because the expense would be charged to only a few individuals (probably the parents of students). We ask to be excused from these requirements.

This petition is forwarded to the Lutheran parish office for an additional report.

The parish office reports to the district office that the Jews in Lichtenau have from time memorial attended the Christian school and participated in all lessons except the religion ones. Therefore there is no formally accepted Jewish elementary teacher and no Jewish elementary school. The religious lessons are taught by a Jewish teacher and cantor in a house owned by the Jewish community. The classroom is on the second floor; third floor in the current English counting system. Although it is small and is not as high as required by law, it is still light, friendly and large enough and because of the classes held in the Christian school, there are never more than 10 Jewish children there at one time. The religion lessons never take so long that the smells may harm one's health. If this is a worry, then a fan may be installed in the window.

The district office reports to the provincial government that the Jews have not presented any plans; and requests that the synagogue council in Lichtenau answer the previous request. The district office reports to the provincial government what the Lutheran parish office has found, and that the Jewish community is unable to pay for any changes.

The Rastatt provincial government returns the files with the decision that changes are not needed. (From Skirball Collection on inspection of Jewish school 1843)

I have included this lengthy extract because it shows us the bureaucratic hurdles Lichtenau faced but more importantly tells us something more about German society – the centrality of rules and regulation, the multiple levels of bureaucracy, the shared responsibility and decision-making among the government and the Lutheran Church and the Jewish community, and the flexibility of multiple paths to achieve the goal, in this case religious and public education for Jewish children. Where they attended public school was ultimately less important than the children receiving a general education, which was seen as an important means of assimilating the Jewish community.

The economic, educational, and political emancipation sought by the Jewish community but ultimately encouraged or limited by government policy and actions was paralleled by the Jewish community's largely self-directed transformation of Judaism from Orthodox to Reform. Judaism began to change in Germany in the late 1700s, driven by the writings of German-Jewish philosopher Moses Mendelssohn (1726-1786), the father of *Haskalah* (the Jewish Enlightenment), and rabbis and scholars who admired his work. He sought to secularize Jewish life and bring Jews into German society, translating the Bible into German (although written in Hebrew), urging toleration, and arguing for the use of reason to reach religious truths. The result was over a half century of considerable religious turmoil in Jewish communities across Germany as Reform (Liberal) Judaism emerged and spread, competing with what was now called Orthodox Judaism and eventually replacing it as the major form of Judaism in Germany. Building on Mendelssohn's writings, the Reform movement is best understood in the contexts of the Enlightenment in Europe and the emancipation process in Germany. As in any transformational movement, there were plenty of competing ideas and personalities, but all reformers shared two basic goals – to make Judaism more compatible with the emerging, modern German society and to preserve Judaism in a modern, Christian world by making Jewish belief and practices comfortable and accessible to all Jews, thereby keeping them within the fold.

The Reform movement emerged and took place mostly in the north. The south had fewer Jews and Jewish communities and, with the exception of Fürth in Franconia, fewer rabbis and scholars. The two leading extreme reformers, Rabbis Abraham Geiger and Samuel Holdheim, held positions in the northern city of Berlin and town of Frankfurt (Oder). German Reform traces its founding to the dedication of a synagogue in Seesen in 17 July 1810. The synagogue was founded by a lay reformer, Israel Jacobson, who simplified and better organized the prayer service and had sermons spoken in German. The synagogue closed after three years and he followed with a second in Berlin. Amid further discussion among reformers, Edward Kley, a follower of Jacobson, founded the Hamburg Temple in 1818. It was the first synagogue to use a Reform liturgy, one of many liturgical reforms to be proposed and adopted over the years.

The Reform movement was riven with conflict. The most basic pitted Reformers against the supporters of Orthodoxy which played out in religion-based division in cities with multiple synagogues and also sometimes drew in the government in response to complaints from Orthodox adherents, thus pitting Reformers against district or city governments. The Reform movement itself was divided between moderate and extreme reformers, with additional theological and strategic fracturing within each group.

Moderate reformers preferred altering religious practices rather than core beliefs. They shortened and simplified the prayer service, replaced individual with communal prayer, expanded participation by women, simplified the ritual calendar, added organs and choirs, preached in German (when they spoke it), and built more elaborate synagogues to rival Christian churches. Extreme reformers instituted the same and similar changes in practice but also and more basically questioned and revised some basic tenets of Judaism including the authority of the Torah and the Talmud, Hebrew as the religious language, Zionism, and celebrating the Sabbath on the seventh day of the week. They also no longer required practices that distinguished Jews from Germans such as circumcision, dietary restrictions (*kashrut*), and rest on the Sabbath. And they looked for a full transformation as they moved beyond belief and practice to alter the rabbinate, which they saw as reflecting an antiquated focus on tradition and ritual, by replacing it with a rabbinate focusing on the theological bases of Judaism, modern issues, and the community rather than individual.

Leaders of the Reform movement recognized that they would be more successful if the different factions compromised and created one, unified movement. Toward that end, rabbis, laypersons, and scholars convened three conferences in the first half of the nineteenth century. The conferences failed to unite reformers nor bring in Orthodox leaders and the effort collapsed with the failed Revolution of 1848. The Revolution was not about Jewish Reform, but many reformers had backed the liberals in the revolution and with the liberal agenda (unification, democracy, worker rights) in disarray and monarchial rule preserved, they saw little future in Germany and several moved on and brought their Reform movement with them to America. With the leadership gone and stronger competition from the emerging Neo-Orthodox movement, the Reform movement in Germany idled; unification conferences in 1869 and 1871 produced agreement only on some moderate reforms and a general agreement that Judaism needed to be compatible with the modern world. Reform rebounded in the late 1800s, but continued to co-exist with Orthodoxy, with many Orthodox in Germany now refugees from Eastern Europe. Judaism in the twentieth century declined across Germany as emancipation and modernity took their toll on religion. Within the first two decades of the century, the percentage of Jews who had left Judaism rose to about twenty-five percent, some becoming secular Jews or atheists and others converting to Christianity and marrying Christians (usually Jewish men converting and marrying Christian women). The children of these marriage were raised as Christians, creating the category of people later labelled *mischlenge* in Nazi Germany.

There were far fewer reformers in Bavaria with its few rabbis and with Fürth as the only major centre of Jewish thought and education. Nonetheless, Reform Judaism came to Uehlfeld early, in about 1808 with the selection of Samson Wolf Rosenfeld as the town's rabbi. His influence extended beyond the town as his election coincided with the Uehlfeld being designated the district rabbinate, consisting over the years of from ten to twelve nearby towns. Rosenfeld was one three reform rabbis with ties to Uehlfeld. The other two were his successor, Isaac Loewi and David Einhorn, who had been born and raised in Diespeck, a member community of the Uehlfeld rabbinate. The reform careers of the three men were quite different and illustrate the several paths Reform took in Germany – acceptance, conflict and co-existence with Orthodoxy, and repression by the government.

11. Photograph of an Etching of Rabbi Samson Wolf Rosenfeld. (Courtesy of the Leo Baeck Institute, New York)

Samson Wolf Rosenfeld was local, born in Uehlfeld in 1783, one of ten children of Hirsch Loew, a cattle dealer, and Sara Rosenfeld. After the usual six years of religious training staring at age thirteen at the *yeshiva* in Fürth he served in Uehlfeld from 1808 until 1826 when he moved on to the prestigious post of rabbi of Bamberg where he served until his death in 1862. Like others, Rosenfeld was influenced by Mendelssohn's writings which led to his advocating moderate reforms. He adhered to the *Halakah* but instituted reforms meant to modernize and secularize the synagogue service including choirs singing in Hebrew and German, organs, a simplified liturgy, shorter services, sermons delivered in High German, a prayer for the Bavarian royal family, and confirmation as a rite for boys and girls. He was one of the first – if not the first rabbi – in Bavaria or perhaps even all of Germany, to deliver sermons in High German rather than Yiddish. His reforms influenced other Bavarian rabbis and won the approval of the government. In his desire to integrate Jews into German life, he adapted the German-Swiss reformer Heinrich Zschokke's (1771-1848) devotional *Stunden der Andacht* (*Hours of Devotion*) for the synagogue. Rosenfeld's adaption, titled *Stunden der Andacht für Israeliten zur Bëforderung religiösen Lebensund häuslicher Gottesverehrung*, was published in four volumes in 1834 and then as a second edition in three volumes in 1838. In 1854 selections were published in Hebrew or Yiddish in Vilna (Vilnius), Lithuania. As with the original work, Rosenfeld's intent was to promote religious nationalism and Enlightenment ideals.

In addition to his rabbinical duties, Rosenfeld also served for many years as the president of the synagogue, a position usually held by a member of the congregation, taught in the school (unusual for rabbis), and directed the design and building of the grand new synagogue which began in 1816 with the synagogue opening in 1818 at 7 Raiffeisenstrasse, at the edge of Jewish neighborhood. Building the new synagogue was an expensive proposition – the final bill came to 11,000 gulden – and the local Jewish communities needed to provide all the funds for the construction and the furnishings. Synagogues built later in the century such as the one in Burghaslach had the benefit of being able to reach beyond the local community and obtain donations from former residents who had migrated to the United States. Rosenfeld so prized the new synagogue that the following year he published a 100-page account of the planning and building process: *Die Israelitische Tempelhalle, Orde die neue Synagoge in Markt Uhlfeld, ihre Entstehung, Einrichtung, und Einweihung* (*The Jewish Temple Hall, or the new Synagogue in Market Uehlfeld, its Development, Establishment, and Inauguration*), in which he explained the religious and civic rationale for the new building:

The old, dilapidated house is unappealing and does not fit in with the now luxurious elements of life in the village and therefore a new synagogue excited the religious citizens. Renovating would not be enough to remedy the deficiencies and an addition would be too large and not serve the purpose. So we had, for our peace of mind and to avoid appearing indifferent to the community, 'no other choice – but to build new!' (Rosenfeld, 1819: S. 1f)

The opening of the new synagogue was a joyous occasion for the Jewish community, celebrated on March fifth and sixth. The celebration on the sixth included musical performances by the choir and then a procession into the synagogue of the schoolchildren, first boys, then girls; the choir directors; fourteen copies of the Bible carried by the rabbi and other men; married men; women; youth; the builder; and spectators.

As the leader of the moderate Reform movement in Bavaria and as a campaigner for Jewish rights we can justifiably label Rosenfeld the most influential Jewish individual born in Uehlfeld. He was succeeded by Isaac Loewi who served from 1826 to 1831. In 1826 the Bavarian government instituted more rigorous educational standards for rabbis including requiring

12. A promotional postcard showing the Lutheran church, synagogue and Haupstarasse in the early 1900s. (Courtesy of Hans Gawronski)

a university education in addition to graduation from a *yeshiva*. Rosenfeld did not have the requisite education and had to pass an exam. Loewi was in the first generation of modern Bavarian rabbis as he meet these standards, having attended yeshiva in Fürth and university in Munich. Loewi was succeeded by Chaim Selz who served from 1832 to 1876. After Selz's death the rabbinate was moved to Fürth, and Uehlfeld no longer had a resident rabbi although like other towns it continued to employ a teacher, cantor, *shochet* and a kosher butcher.

Loewi continued Rosenfeld's moderate reforms until he was elected to the prestigious post of Rabbi of Fürth where he served until 1873. His first ten years in Fürth were more difficult than his time in Uehlfeld as he battled opposition and efforts to remove him by Orthodox members of the community. The conflicts were never fully resolved and the Reform and Orthodox came to co-exist:

> Yet in one crucial respect the Jewish community of Fürth was divided: between a Reform or Liberal minority and an Orthodox majority. Proponents of Reform like Isaak Loewi, who became chief rabbi in 1831, wished (among other things) that Jewish worship should conform more to the style of Christian worship. Under his influence, the main synagogue was given a more church like layout, with standing desks replaced by pews, and the addition of an organ in 1873; worshippers no longer wore 'tallit'… But the majority of Fürth Jews reacted against the Reform movement. Thus, while the liberal congregation controlled the main synagogue, other smaller synagogues around the 'schulhof' were the domain of Orthodoxy. The division extended into the realm of education. The children of Reform Jews attended the public gymnasium or the Girls' Lyceum, along with their gentile contemporaries, while the children of the Orthodox families were sent to the Jewish high school (Realchule) at 31 31 Blumenstrasse where there no Saturday classes. (Ferguson, 2015)

As chief rabbi, Loewi stuck with the Reform agenda and also became a leading citizen of Bavaria and a favorite of King Ludwig II who visited the synagogue and asked Loewi to bless him in 1869.

The third Uehlfeld-connected reformer, David Einhorn (1809-1879) took a much different path and found himself caught in the disapproving vise of religious and regional politics. Unlike the moderate Rosenfeld and Loewi, Einhorn was an extreme reformer, a follower of Berlin's Abraham Geiger, although Einhorn had been educated in the Orthodox tradition at the same yeshiva in Fürth as Rosenfeld and Loewi. District governments across Germany monitored their Jewish communities and their Reform movement and several encouraged reform but some and especially in Bavaria accepted moderate Reform but were wary of any major changes and especially those which brought complaints from leading Jewish citizens wishing to retain Orthodoxy. For conservative government officials these complaints were worrisome and unwelcome signs of unrest in the Jewish community and officials sometimes intervened to curtail extreme reforms. David Einhorn was one those who found his reforms and actions the subjects of complaints, which led more than one district or city government to ban his reforms and force him to resign. His troubles began in 1838 when he was appointed rabbi of Wellhausen. But, as we saw with the teacher Rosenthal in Lichtenau, these appointments required several levels of local and district approval and government objections to his appointment delayed it until 1847. Once installed, he moved ahead with his reforms but was rebuked by the government several times, most seriously for blessing an uncircumcised boy in the synagogue. Frustrated by Orthodox and government resistance, and also the failure of revolution of 1848, Einhorn moved on to Pest, Hungary. But, there too, some congregants found him too extreme and his synagogue was shut down in just two months. In 1855 he gave up on Germany and moved to the United States and established a rabbinical position in Baltimore. He took his reform and liberal political agenda with him and was soon at odds with Rabbi Isaac Mayer Wise (1819-1900), a more moderate reformer in Cincinnati. But his debates with Wise looked peaceful after Einhorn was driven out of Baltimore by angry slavery supporters after he delivered a sermon supporting abolitionism. He fled to Philadelphia and led a synagogue there and later one in New York. All the while he continued to advocate for extreme reforms (but not intermarriage with Christians), reinterpreted basic theology, and contributed liturgical innovations, gaining supporters and contributing major innovations to the American Reform movement.

Circling back to the Rindsbergs, we dip back into family history again to open our discussion of another major element of the Jewish experience during emancipation – immigration from rural areas to the cities and to America. We know that David Feist, the youngest of the first three 'Rindsberg' men was my mother's direct lineal ancestor. He lived his adult life during the early decades of the emancipation process, but died before Jews were fully emancipated across Germany in 1871. He married twice. We never found the name of his first wife. His second wife was Ella Hecht and they were married in 1829. David Feist Rindsberg had at least four children, two with his anonymous first wife: Jacob in either 1800 or 1804, Feist David in 1813, and two with Ella: Regina in 1831 and Joseph David in 1835. Jacob

Rindsberg immigrated to Cincinnati, Ohio, initiating the chain migration to America of several Rindsbergs during the 1800s which produced a sizeable contingent of Rindsberg descendants in southern Ohio. Cincinnati was a popular destination for Jewish German immigrants in the decades before the Civil War and by 1860 they constituted half of the city's Jewish population. Cincinnati was desirable because it was a growing city in a convenient location on the Ohio River and America's largest interior city west of the Alleghenies. It provided the opportunity for Jewish German immigrants to succeed in America by transferring their trading experience into shop-keeping and to build on their involvement in the garment industry, but now as manufacturers rather than traders.

The second son by the first marriage, Feist David, was my mother's next direct lineal ancestor, her great-grandfather. He married Regina Katz in 1834 and they had at least ten children, four sons and six daughters born between 1843 and 1862. Two children, Babette and Joseph, followed their uncle Jacob to America and the two youngest children, Marie and Jacob, moved to Cologne and Fürth. The other six children evidently also remained in Germany, but in accord with the Edict's restrictions on Jewish residence, only one son, David Feist, the youngest son, remained in Uehlfeld.

These Rindsbergs who sought a better life in America were part of a massive emigration from Germany to the United States from about 1820 through 1880. During that period nearly five million Germans immigrated to the 'Golden Land'. They settled mainly in the Midwest but also in cities in the east. The 1850s was a decade of heavy emigration with nearly one million Germans leaving for America (there was really no other place with opportunity to move to), topped only by the 1880s with one and half million heading across the Atlantic. Among these immigrants were about 150,000 Jews. In both groups, immigration was heaviest from the south and southwest of Germany, rural areas most susceptible to economic downturns and political unrest. These rural folk moved on mainly because of a rapid decrease in the amount of land available for farming, the predictable result of inheritance customs which split land among several heirs, leaving many heirs with economically unsustainable holdings. The crop failures of 1816 (known as the 'Year without Summer' in the United States and Europe because of the cold weather and snow) and 1844-46 further pushed Germans to seek their futures in America. Beyond the economic push factors was political unrest, particularly the disputes between liberals and conservatives, resulting in the failed Revolution of 1848. The unrest and violence and the survival of the monarchy hardly reassured citizens that Germany was on a smooth or fast path to democracy or unification.

Few Jews farmed, but they were part of and dependent on the farm economy and many supported the liberals in the revolution, so they too had economic and political reasons to leave. It is estimated that about 25,000 Bavarian Jews immigrated to the U.S. between 1800 and 1871, about fifteen percent of Jews who immigrated in those years. But as with most everything in Jewish German experience, Jews had their own additional push out of Germany, the provision of the Edict of 1813 which made permission to reside in a community not heritable, meaning that only one son of the family could continue to live there, and only if he could show that he had an occupation and could support his family. Other sons had to move to their wife's community and take over her father's business, or not marry and live with their parents, or immigrate to cities or the United States or elsewhere such as France or England. Daughters could either live with their husband or move to cities or outside Germany.

The Edict along with other developments such as industrialization and emigration had some of its intended effects. The size of the Jewish community in Bavaria was controlled, increasing from 53,208 in 1813 to only 57,498 in 1848, making the Jews an even smaller minority as the German population increased by 25 per cent over the same time span. The major change came in the Jewish settlement pattern as they became more urban, with 30 per cent of Jews living in Bavarian cities in 1871 as compared to only 14 per cent in 1840. Jewish occupations changed as well. By 1849 the per cent who were identified as peddlers – a major target of the Edict's economic reforms – had dropped to 6 per cent. Most Jews were now involved in the wholesale and retail trades or were craftsmen, although involvement in the crafts would decline later in the century. Farming did not catch on as some like Rabbi Rosenfeld expected and by 1848 only 8 per cent farmed compared to seventy-eight of Germans who farmed or as in the past combined farming with crafts.

To sum up, when Germany became a unified nation in 1871 all Jews across Germany were fully emancipated, although anti-Semitism and discrimination persisted and continued to limit Jewish participation in German society. Nonetheless, Jewish life had been transformed over the century and while they remained a tiny minority they were moving to substantial economic and political integration in German society and that integration would only broaden and deepen over the next decades.

7

Freedom and Opportunity

David Feist Rindsberg, the son who stayed in Uehlfeld, was my mother's maternal grandfather. Born in 1855, he came of age during the final years of the emancipation process. As the youngest son he was the one who remained in Uehlfeld (more often it was the oldest son) and took over his father's cattle business and the family home. Emancipation also meant that he was eligible for military service and he proudly served, as a cavalryman in King Ludwig II's Bavarian Army from 1875 to 1878. David married Lina Sturm in 1884. David and Lina Rindsberg evidently thought highly of King Ludwig and named their third child, Ludwig, after the king. Such naming was not unusual, as assimilating Jewish parents were drifting away from the tradition of giving all their children ancestral names and instead gave some of their children German names.

The family story is that it was David's military service that led to his meeting Lina Sturm and their marriage. Supposedly, they met when David was billeted in Lina's family's Burghaslach home. He fell madly in love with her and ardently wooed her. This tale of David's and Lina's first meeting may be true, but when considered in the context of German marital practices at the time, it is conceivable, even probable, that it was an arranged or semi-arranged marriage. In Germany, romantic love as the basis for marriage did not begin replacing arranged marriage until the 1870s and then first in the cities and only gradually in rural areas. This is hardly unusual in the human history where some form of arranged marriage involving economic transfers from one family to another (dowry, bride price, bride service) has often been the norm. Arranged marriage, of course, can take a variety of forms from a formal, ritualized negotiation between the fathers to a not-so-subtle push by the parents to get their children, who already knew one another, together. I think a case can be made that David and Lina's was one these semi-arranged marriages, as probably were many marriages. Uehlfeld's civil records show us that Burghaslach was a source of brides for Uehlfeld men in the 1800s, with at least five young Uehlfeld men marrying Burghaslach women. A look at a Middle Franconia map tells us why. Burghaslach is only ten miles northwest of Uehlfeld; Burghaslacher Strasse leading out of Uehlfeld in that direction. In addition, Burghaslach had a sizeable Jewish population, and was served by the Uehlfeld rabbinate, producing regular contact among Jews from the two towns. But proximity would not have been enough as arranged marriages were economic relationships based on the dowry, the customary transfer of money or goods from the bride's family through the bride to the groom. The dowry provided some economic stability for a young couple. Lina may well have brought a decent dowry. Her father was a tanner and leather dealer even before emancipation and was very likely wealthier than David's cattle dealer father. Marriage arrangement also created social, economic, and political alliances between families. This may have mattered to the Sturms and Rindsbergs as the families probably had a business relationship as the Rindsbergs may have supplied the Sturms with cattle or hides. So, there is consistent though circumstantial evidence that it was semi-arranged marriage. Of course, it was not unusual for arranged marriages to really be semi-arranged as the young man and woman already knew and desired each other and this was probably true for David and Lina.

We visited Burghaslach the same day as Uehlfeld and the two towns looked much alike. Not surprisingly, so too where their Jewish histories. Burghaslach once had a sizeable Jewish population which decreased in the late 1800s as Jews moved to America and German cities. The town was probably first settled by Franks moving east in the 700s. From the late sixteenth century to 1806, all or some portion of the town was ruled by the Counts of Castell and portions at times also by the Baron of Muenster. The first Jewish residents were servants of the ruling families and in the 1700s the noble built at least two *Judenhaus* – dwellings divided into apartments – for the Jewish residents, suggesting that he wanted Jews to remain in town. By the end of the century, Jews owned their own homes. In 1722 there were 25 Jewish families (about 120 individuals) and by 1783 the population had increased to 251 individuals. The Jewish population remained relatively stable until the 1850s and 1860s when migration to cities such as Fürth and Nuremberg and to the United States accelerated. In 1833 the Jewish population had been 254; by 1888 it was down to 187 and then it declined further to 109 in 1902, 80 in 1920, and 60 in 1933 when the Nazis came to power.

The Burghaslach Jewish community built its first synagogue in the early 1700s on land owned by the Baron of Muenster. In 1731 the community opened its own synagogue – a single room on the back of a house. In 1870, after fifteen years of planning and fund-raising, the community built a new, larger synagogue on the town's main street and renovated it in 1912 to keep up appearances with the recently renovated Lutheran Church. The community had also built a school in 1858, behind the synagogue. It remained in use as the Jewish public school until 1924 when it closed due to too few pupils. A cemetery was established in town in 1775. Thus, the Burghaslach Jewish community history was much like Uehlfeld's although it was ruled by different families.

The Burghaslach Sturm genealogy has been well-documented by the late Thea Skyte, a Sturm descendant in England. The first of Lina Sturm's ancestors Thea found in Burghaslach was a man known as Schmul who lived there in the early to mid-1700s. His son, Eisig Samuel, lived in the town in the middle to the late 1700s. He was a tanner and leather dealer, two relatively prestigious occupations for small-town Jewish men. His son, Löw Eisig, was the first in Burghaslach to take the Sturm surname. He was a cattle dealer and after his father's death took over the tanning business. A letter of protection he received on 22 November 1798 required that his father's 'protection' would be transferred to him on the condition 'that he carries on with the tannery trade, as his father had done'. He married a woman named Babette and they had five children, one of the sons, Solomon, being the direct ancestor of my mother. In 1872 Solomon was appointed to a three-year term as cantor of the new synagogue in Burghaslach. He married Hanna Hecht and the couple had four children, the youngest being my mother's grandmother Lina, born in 1858. Following his father's tradition of service to the Jewish community, son Isaac served as the community's *shochet* for several years while another son Joseph immigrated to Baltimore in the 1880s following his uncle Samuel.

Rural Jewish men either married women from their own town or like David Rindsberg, women from another town who usually then moved to the husband's town. Lina moved to Uehlfeld where David would eventually inherit his father's cattle business. David and Lina had thirteen children, eight of whom lived to adulthood, an unusually large number of children for a Jewish family in Bavaria at the time. Demographic data shows that the size of Jewish families in Bavaria declined over the nineteenth century and fertility data shows that couples like David and Lina who married between 1871 and 1924 had an average of only 2.9 children. Why David and Lina had thirteen children is not known. Among the eight children who lived to adulthood were my mother's mother Rosa, born in 1897 and her brother Julius, born in 1896, who enters our story in Chapter 10.

The family lived in a three-storey stucco house at 3 Raiffeisenstrasse, in what had been the Jewish neighbourhood. The synagogue and Jewish school were just around the corner. Behind the house was a courtyard and a stone barn, with a chicken coop in front. David either owned or rented a pasture, a half-block away across the River Aisch. Hanging into the river lashed to posts secured on the bank were wooden fish boxes where David and other men kept fish they had caught to be harvested later. He was known in town as 'der Langer' as he was tall and thin and the family as 'der Langers' to distinguish them from the family of Hirsch and Rika Rindsberg who lived next door. David and Hirsch were best friends and distant cousins, although by the 1920s descendants of the three Rindsberg brothers no longer considered themselves to be relatives. Hirsch owned a store in town that sold grain and other farm supplies and equipment to local farmers. As we saw, David Rindsberg served in the Bavarian army as a cavalryman and his sons Ludwig, Felix, and Julius served in the First World War . Military service was especially important as it marked one as a full citizen of Germany. The family was proud of David's service and a portrait of him in uniform, mounted on his horse hung prominently over the sofa in the living room. David Rindsberg was an active member of the community. He spoke German, not Yiddish, was a member of the town's veteran's organization and a regular player in the village-wide Saturday evening card games. In the evening after securing the cattle in the barn behind the house, he and his friend Hirsch enjoyed a pitcher of beer, which my mother happily fetched for him from one of the town's three breweries when she visited in the summers.

All of David and Lina's eight children were born after emancipation and grew up in a Germany very different from that of their parents. This post-emancipation generation grew up with freedom and opportunity nearly equal to that afforded Christian Germans. But there were limitations from the past linked in various ways to ongoing transformations of German society that continued to limit and channel Jewish life.

Historians divide the Germany of the post-emancipation decades into two political periods. First, the German Empire (Second Reich) from 1871 to 1919 marked by political consolidation and autocratic rule, alliance with Austria and then Italy, and Germany's emergence as a European power fuelled by rapid industrialization, militarization, and colonialism in Africa and the Pacific. The empire dissolved with Germany's defeat in the First World War and the harsh terms of the Treaty of Versailles. Replacing it was the second period, the democratic but politically and economically unstable Weimer Republic. Political instability came from sometimes violent conflict between communists, socialists, liberal democrats, and the right-wing NSDAP and other, smaller parties. Economic instability was the inevitable result of the harsh reparations requirements of the Treaty of Versailles, inflation, and then the Great Depression which badly damaged Germany's economy.

The political and economic changes during these two periods was accompanied by a rise in anti-Semitism, although historians do not agree

13. Julius Rindsberg mounted during his cavalry service during the First World War.

about all aspects of anti-Semitism during these years. It does seem clear, though, that there was a shift in intellectual circles from religion-based to racial anti-Semitism and increasing resentment especially among some small businessmen about Jewish economic success and among some intellectuals about Jewish prominence in the sciences, medicine, and the arts. While Jewish rights were supported by the government, anti-Semitism emerged on the agendas of several minor political parties and was evident in formal social interactions, with Jews excluded from many private organizations. The combination of new opportunity and continuing resistance to equality and full participation in German society led Jews to expand existing and establish their own educational, social, and charitable organizations usually under the auspices of the local Jewish community. Thus, as in the past, Jews in significant ways remained outside German society, although in other ways such as education, business, and military service, they were highly integrated.

Anti-Jewish sentiment had only limited effect on Jewish economic progress as economic and even limited political emancipation freed Jews to live where they wanted, own land, open or expand wholesale and retail operations, establish factories, attend university, and work in the professions. Many Jewish traders moved to larger towns or cities and opened wholesale operations, retail stores, factories and distribution companies. Some sons and sometimes daughters then took over these businesses later in the century while others choose to attend university and enter the professions. Not only did Jews expand their businesses but they also broadened their markets. Taking advantage of new efficiencies brought by the Industrial Revolution including railroads, in the mid-nineteenth century some Jewish manufacturers and merchants moved from primarily local to urban, then regional, then European, and finally international markets.

In addition to Jewish businessmen and their families, many young, single, small-town Jewish and German men and women also headed to cities like Berlin, Frankfurt, Bamberg, Fürth, Munich and Nuremburg where there they found better employment and education opportunities and marriage prospects. David and Lina's children joined the stream. Daughters Elsa, Gutta, Johanna and Rosa all moved to Frankfurt and Flora moved to Nuremburg. Ludwig married a woman named Meta Blum and the couple settled in Konigsberg while Feist Felix married a woman named Selma Stuehler and they lived in her hometown of Adelsdorf where he joined her father's cattle business. Only David and Lina's youngest son Julius remained in Uehlfeld where he worked in the cattle business with his father and may have also traded in horses. Like many small towns that once had large Jewish populations, Uehlfeld, too, was no longer a 'Jewish' town; the Jewish population declined to 80 in 1910, 70 in 1924, 33 in 1930, 15 in 1938 and then one after November 1938. The decline in the 1930s was not about searching for a better life in the cities but was caused by harassment by local and regional Nazi supporters and officials meant to drive Jews from Germany.

Of course, not all Jews left their small towns in the late 1800s and early 1900s and some who stayed improved their economic positions and a few became wealthy, at least by rural standards. Most successful were Jewish families who bought land and went into farming and leasing land to Germans, hops dealers in the rapidly expanding hops market, and retail merchants who opened general stores. Not all were successful and less well-off were the elderly or those who remained in traditional Jewish occupations such as small-scale cattle dealing and butchering.

Jews who stayed in Uehlfeld typified this pattern. In 1891, three of the five wealthiest men in town were Jewish – Julius, Sigmund, and David Dingfelder. The Dingfelders wealth came from the land; they farmed their own land, rented farm land to Germans, and boarded horses. Including these three Dingfelders, 11 of the 25 wealthiest families in town were Jewish. The 1913 tax list shows an even greater concentration of town wealth in Jewish families, although more aggregate wealth remained in the hands of their more numerous German neighbors, most of whom were still farmers. As in 1891, the three wealthiest men in town were Jewish – Emil Dingfelder, farmer and landowner, Mortiz Gutherz, hops merchant and Ignatz Schwab, merchant.

As mentioned earlier, two of the traditional economic bedrocks of Jewish rural life, cattle dealing and hops trading, were both markedly transformed beginning in the middle of the 1800s as the combination of emancipation, movement to cities, industrialization, improvements in communication and transportation technology (railroads), and a growing European and international economic order made it possible and more profitable to expand operations and one's territory. Cattle dealing became an international business with some cattle dealers now operating large import/export operations across national boundaries. This new breed of cattle dealers were modern entrepreneurs who employed non-Jews, serviced multiple markets, and became wealthy. Business expansion and consolidation led to a twenty-five percent decrease in the overall number of Jewish cattle dealers in Germany between 1882 and 1914 although most small towns still had at least one small-scale Jewish cattle dealer in the 1920s. Those dealers were often among the least wealthy residents of the towns, although they enjoyed some security because the German farmers had no other means to get their cattle to market.

The hops trade underwent its own transformation, from a regional to an international business and, as with the cattle trade, Jewish traders drove the transition, growing their businesses in some cases into large international trading houses. Franconia's Jewish hops dealers were especially well-positioned to take advantage of the new opportunities when Nuremberg emerged in the 1840s as Central Europe's leading hops exchange, with nearby Fürth and Bamberg developing companion exchanges. Nuremberg was ideally positioned, located in the center of Bavaria's most productive hops-growing region, the hub for towns in all directions which for centuries had grown and traded hops. Nuremberg was also ideally positioned on the railroad for regional and later international trade; Germany's first steam-powered railway, the Bavarian Ludwig Railway, began service, traveling the six miles from Nuremberg to Fürth in 1835. The hops trade expanded rapidly when the international market opened up in 1858, made possible by the German government allowing preservation by sulfurization in 1858 for export (and then in 1862 for sale in Germany). By the 1860s Nuremberg housed a thriving hops exchange and dozens of wholesale trading houses, some owned by Christians who saw and acted on the new opportunity, others by Jews who likewise saw the opportunity and relocated to Nuremberg from nearby hops-producing towns like Uehlfeld, building on their generations of trade relationships as middlemen between Germans farmers and breweries. The arrival of these Jewish traders and other Jews looking for new possibilities made Nuremberg the center of Jewish life in Bavaria, a dramatic reversal of opportunity for, as we saw, Nuremberg had expelled its Jewish population in 1499 and destroyed its cemetery, planning to never let Jews return. Jews did return and their community grew from eighty-seven people in mid-century to over 3,000 in 1880 and then over 9,000 by 1933. The growth and influence of the Jewish community was part of Nuremberg's rapid emergence as Bavaria's second-largest city after Munich, its population increasing from only 56,000 1850 to over 400,000 in 1930.

One of those who took advantage of the expanding hops market and with other dealers, both Jewish and Christian, drove the growth of the hops trade and the city was Loeb Hopf, a native of Uehlfeld. Born into a hops-trading family in the early years of emancipation Hopf had been a fur trader, a more lucrative business than hops trading at the time. In 1828, he received permission to open a kosher restaurant in Uehlfeld, apparently sensing that new economic opportunities might produce more disposable income for some Jewish families in town and for visitors. Such restaurants and Jewish-owned inns were not unusual, as Jewish travelers needed places to stay where they could get a kosher meal. What came of the restaurant is not known, but he also began trading hops in the 1830s, and either the restaurant or the hops business or both proved successful. By 1848 he had become the wealthiest Jewish man in town, with assets of 70,000 fl., 20,000 fl. more than the next two wealthiest men, one also a hops dealer, the other a general merchant. Seeing more room for expansion in the city, Hopf relocated to Nuremburg in 1852 where he opened his wholesale hops trading house, Hopf & Soehne, with his two sons. They made the business a success and when the international market opened, they quickly took the opportunity, becoming what today would be called commodities traders, loaning money to farmers before the growing season and speculating that market prices would be high enough to make a decent profit later in the year. Loeb Hopf also took a leading role in Nuremberg's rapidly growing Jewish community, becoming the first president of its council. But the Nuremberg hops trade could not last forever and by the early twentieth century, with the United States now a major grower and distributor of hops, the German trade declined leading to acquisitions and mergers in Nuremberg and elsewhere and a reduced role for Jewish traders.

While most attention has been given to the rural to urban population and economic flow, it is important to note, as German historian Stefanie Fischer points out, that the flow was not entirely rural to urban as some merchants, hops dealers, and others relocated their operations from small towns to nearby larger towns where there were more customers and quicker transport to cities. For example, the Schwab family, merchants in Uehlfeld, had become successful by 1848, with three family members having combined assets of 90,000 fl. The family also had a store in Neustadt, ten miles down the Aisch, in the 1890s which remained prosperous until the 1930s. By the late 1800s many businesses like the Schwab's general stores, as well as chain stores, local markets, and book, art, antique, and second-hands shops were often owned by Jews. In the 1890s Jews introduced department stores to Germany, following the American department store model (for example, Gimbels, Macy's, Bloomingdale's, Kauffman's) pioneered earlier by immigrant Jewish German traders who had succeeded in the United States.

By 1900 this rural to urban flow combined with the new economic and educational opportunities had transformed Germany's Jewish population from a largely rural, poor minority to a largely urban, middle and upper-middle class minority. Jews had made greater educational and economic progress than their German contemporaries, who remained largely rural and did not begin making their own rapid educational and economic gains until the early twentieth century.

Their new political freedom combined with their wealth also gave Jews more political influence in towns as the number of votes a man could cast depended on how much he paid in taxes. In 1897, the nineteen Jewish men in Uehlfeld eligible to vote held a total of seventy-one votes. But the seventy-four Christians had a combined 131 votes, meaning that Jews as a group remained a political minority. In the May, 1913 referendum on the town budget, Julius Dingfelder had 14 votes to cast. Most other citizens, Jewish and German, had only one or two votes. Emancipation meant also that Jews could live anywhere in town and some moved out of the old, Jewish neighborhood in Uehlfeld, although most remained there in houses that had been in their families for several generations.

One of the most contentious questions about the Holocaust is to what extent did average German citizens participate in the killing of Jews and the destruction of European Jewish communities. Behind this question is a more basic one – just what was the relationship among Germans and Jews before the rise of the Nazi Party? As the Nazi Party drew some of its earliest and strongest support in Middle Franconia, what we can learn about the extent and nature of pre-Holocaust Jewish-German relations in Uehlfeld may help answer this question.

Unfortunately *may* is the operative word, as it is a very difficult topic to address. From documents we do know a good bit about trading and moneylending relationships and other economic relationships as well as civic and political ones, but social relations between Jews and Germans are poorly described. Official records don't mention meetings on the street, gossip passed during trade negotiations, or banter at the weekly market. In addition to being a difficult issue, it is also a complex one as interaction between Jews and Germans took place across several domains: business, politics, civic life, voluntary associations, religion, education, military service, marriage and family, and social. In addition, interaction varied over time and place. Here we look at Jewish-German relations is small towns, locales where everyone knew or at least knew of one another and where some families – both Jewish and German had lived for several generations. In this setting we find a degree of familiarity and personal knowledge among residents often absent in cities.

It seems helpful to begin by noting three general patterns in Jewish-German relations across Germany. First, whether Germans knew Jews and how they knew them varied widely. Many Germans did not personally know and had little or no interaction with Jews, because there were no Jews living in their town or the region. For other Germans, who lived in towns with Jewish populations like Uehlfeld, there was regular interaction, in the streets and at the market. And in regions like Franconia where there were large Jewish populations in some towns and cities and no Jews in others, many Germans encountered only Jews who were traders and peddlers, and were considered an undesirable element. Second, because many Germans lacked personal knowledge of Jews, their image of Jews was typically a negative, ethnocentric stereotype in which German culture and Christianity were seen as far superior to Jewish culture and Judaism and Jews were seen as all of one type. That type is graphically described in the petition quoted from below; a petition objecting to Jewish equality sent to the Bavarian parliament in

1849 from the town of Hirschau in the Upper Palatinate, a predominately Catholic region in which Jews constituted only .2 per cent of the population.

> We can speak from experience. For many years a Jew by the name of 'Luber' from Hüttenbach, has managed, despite many protestations of the local tradespeople, to secure his residence; and how that man plies his haggling trade! He lurks constantly at the gates of our town and tries to make some deal with anyone entering; he forever makes the rounds of pubs and private homes, solely to press his wares on people; if a spendthrift housewife, a faithless servant, a son in need of ready money, or such a daughter wants to get hold of money quickly, one pays a visit to the Jew and gets from him what is wanted, to be sure at a very sad extra charge. If business is not good in town, he takes a pack full of goods and goes with it into surrounding villages, where he keeps pressing the local inhabitants until finally a deal is made; and he takes anything, even stolen goods, in place of payment, knowing how to resell everything through his connections; thus any influx of business from the outside is cut off to local tradespeople, because these will, can, and ought not slink about the countryside and in town, but rather earn their living by work and the pursuit of agriculture. (Harris 1994: 254)

The third general feature of Jewish-German relations was that these relations were unbalanced, despite the belief of the people of Hirschau and elsewhere that even Jewish peddlers had the upper hand when it came to financial dealings and if there were too many of them they would quickly take over the local economy. The reality was that Germans typically held the upper hand and even while poor peasants might find themselves dependent at times on Jewish moneylenders, they also knew that they, the peasants, had the backing of the rulers and church and that if they suffered too much new laws would be enacted restricting the Jewish business activities they objected to. Or, they could deal with the matter directly, and physically beat the Jewish trader or peddler into agreement.

Turning now to nature of Jewish-German interactions, we can begin by noting that throughout most of the 1800 or so years Jews have lived in Germany, interaction between Jews and Germans was mainly about buying from and selling to the other. And because Jews until the nineteenth century had no political power, Jewish interaction with the ruler and his agents was also primarily a business relationship, with the ruler enabling Jews to earn a living and Jews providing revenue through their payments of taxes and fees.

In the other spheres of interaction, Jews and Germans lived largely separate lives, often in separate neighbourhoods in town. They did not intermarry, share or convert to each other's religions, Jews were mostly excluded from civic and political life, and their children went to separate schools when possible. Conversion and intermarriage was so rare until emancipation that for all of the eighteenth century in Uehlfeld, I found only one Jewish woman and no men converted to Lutheranism; she married a Christian man, and moved away.

Perhaps the main venues for interaction beyond business negotiations were the taverns where Jewish and German men drank beer and the weekly market. There was occasional hostility reflected in verbal and physical quarrels, the occasional vandalizing of Jewish cemeteries and synagogues, but no large-scale harassment or violence, other than the Hep! Hep! riots in 1819 since the expulsions of the sixteenth and seventeenth centuries.

Jewish distance from their German neighbours was both symbolized and reinforced by Jews speaking a different language for about seven hundred years. Their language was Yiddish which emerged as a distinct language with several regional dialects spoken by a distinct people (Jews), in Central Europe between 900 and 1100. The Yiddish spoken in Germany was Western Yiddish and was close to German. The Yiddish spoken later in Eastern Europe was Eastern Yiddish, with more Slavic vocabulary than Western Yiddish. A third, variant, South Yiddish, showed Hungarian and Balkan influences. Linguists classify Western Yiddish as a Germanic language as 75 per cent of its vocabulary is German, the remainder taken mainly from Hebrew. It is written in the Hebrew alphabet. Because of the overlap in vocabulary, Yiddish and German were to some extent mutually intelligible in some locales including Franconia and Yiddish or the trade dialect *Lachoudisch* or Judeo-German, based on Yiddish and German, was often the language used by Jewish traders and their German suppliers and customers. As Jews moved from Central to Eastern Europe, the conventional wisdom is that Yiddish went with them where it became Eastern Yiddish, the daily language of Jews in Russia, Poland, Lithuania and they then brought the language to America, where it eventually fell out of widespread use but developed a nostalgic and romanticized image as a reminder of an earlier period in Jewish life. Jews also had a different religious language – Hebrew – than their Christian neighbours. Yiddish began to decline in German Jewish communities in the late 1700s, although more slowly in the rural areas than in the cities. The movement toward emancipation in the early 1800s speeded its near disappearance as Jews sought to become full participants in German life. By the last decades of the 1800s, German, not Yiddish, was spoken and written in Jewish homes in

Uehlfeld. My mother's grandparents spoke German, in a Bavarian dialect. Nonetheless, in rural areas, some Yiddish words remained in use into the twentieth century as a trade language. Select Yiddish terms also remained in use in Jewish homes into the 1930s just as English-speaking Jews and non-Jews in the United States continue to use Yiddish words and phrases in the twenty-first century.

Emancipation expanded the opportunities for Jewish-German interaction as it broadened the role of Jews in German society. Political participation came earlier in the north than in the south where early in the emancipation period Jews could now vote and hold public office and serve in the military, although informal restrictions remained in place. Acceptance of Jews in small towns was perhaps made easier because they were no longer a large minority, as many had moved to cities or America. Many Germans had moved as well and some activities required cooperation among all residents. One of those was the volunteer fire department (Freiwilligen Feuerwehr (FFW), a small town's foremost voluntary organization charged with combatting the town's fiercest enemy. In Uehlfeld, the Jewish community was actively involved in its founding in August, 1869. Ten Jewish men were among its sixty founding members – Ignatz Schwab; Louis Wahle; Israel, Max, Julius, Solomon, and Wolf Rindsberg; and Sigmund, Maier, and Seligman Dingfelder. Schwab served as the department's secretary from 1869 to 1871, holding the dual if dubious honor of being both the first and last Jewish man to hold a leadership position in the department. The Jewish community also donated '7 fire escapes woven by the hands of Jews themselves, value 14 fl.' And 150 meters of blue cloth were ordered from textile merchant Martin Wahle for the uniforms.

The FFW faced its greatest challenge on 25 May 1888 when the town suffered its worst destruction since the Thirty Years' War, some 250 years earlier. A fire consumed dozens of buildings including the synagogue, Jewish school, and dozens of houses and barns including several Jewish homes. The fire followed by a month another large conflagration on 29 April. Hirsch Rindsberg, whose house at 5 Raiffeisenstrasse abutted the synagogue, noted in his prayer book: 'On the afternoon of May 25, 1888, a fierce fire broke out and reduced to ashes 62 dwellings and related buildings, including the synagogue and school building.' Three days after the fire, Hirsch's neighbour and my mother's great-grandfather, Feist David Rindsberg, sent a note to the town council thanking the fire company from nearby Höchstadt for its 'energetic and spirited help' which saved his ice box and other property and wishing that 'May God protect them from such horrors.' All of the buildings were rebuilt through a town-wide effort in two years. The Jewish community raised the funds to rebuild the synagogue and the school, with the synagogue on the existing footprints, using the surviving walls and recreating the original design elements.

Military service like fire department service was important to the Jewish community as it signified citizenship and also they hoped proved that Jews were patriotic and loyal Germans. Several Jewish men served in the Bavarian army and three of them – my mother's grandfather David Rindsberg and Samuel and Sigmund Dingfelder – were members of the town's veterans association in the early 1900s.

Some German Jews served in the Franco-Prussian War (1870-71) but it was the First World War that provided the first major opportunity after emancipation for Jews to prove their patriotism; some 100,000 German Jews fought for Germany; 12,000 were killed. This was a higher percentage of participation than by the German population as a whole, although it did not stop some from claiming during and after the war that Jews did not do their share. Uehlfeld's Jewish population did its share; twenty-three men served in the German army, twenty-one at the front. Among the soldiers were the three sons of David and Lina Rindsberg – Ludwig, Felix, and Julius. Felix's service record shows that he saw considerable action; he was at the battles of the Somme and Aisne, in the battles between the Meuse and the Moselle, at Flanders and at battles at the Marne and Champagne and between Reims and Soissons. Two of the Jewish soldiers were killed in action and five were wounded. The two men who were killed – Lieut. Alfred Dingfelder and Infantryman Siegfried Rindsberg are memorialised with their names placed along with those of German men killed in the war on the memorial in front of the Lutheran church. Although during the Nazi era, efforts were made to remove all signs of Jewish life in Uehlfeld, the names of these two men were left untouched on the memorial. This is in contrast to some other towns where the names of Jewish men were scratched from the First World War memorials. An obituary for Alfred Dingfelder appeared in the German-Jewish newspaper, *The Israelite*, on 5 August 1915, which gives us some insight into Jewish notions of patriotism and national service.

> The family of Mr. Emil Dingfelder was affected by a heavy loss by the death on July 25, of the eldest son of Mr. Dingfelder, Lieutenant Alfred Dingfelder who fell in the struggle for the fatherland. The hero had a short military career yet was so rich in deeds.
>
> On December 8, last year, he was called up for military service. In late January he took to the field. In a short time there, he acquired the trust and satisfaction of his superiors to the degree that he was assigned to an officer course before mid-February. After six weeks of training, he received there the officer's commission. As handsome

officer he spent thereon a six-day vacation with his dear parents. It was the last stay in his parent's home. On Erev Pesach on he had to go back to his troops. After a short period on the Eastern Front, he went a few weeks ago to the Vosges Mountains. Through his courageous valor, fidelity to duty and comradely behavior, he brings honor to all of Judaism. In the afternoon of July 25, at 3 3/4 clock, he took a fatal bullet. He is buried in close proximity to the place where he endured the greatest hardships and sacrificed his life for all of us. His battalion commander reported that he was extremely popular because of his kindness and efficiency: 'He made us all proud and performed with bravery and bold energy during the heaviest shelling. We are the valuable comrades who will never forget. Condolences to his hard-hit family. May the All-Merciful comfort the grieving parents and relatives.'

Although there seems to have been more informal social contact between Germans and Jews in small towns after emancipation, one customary form of entertainment and interaction which brought men together regularly was the *stammtisch*:

Men gathered [in taverns or cafes] during the evenings primarily to play cards and drink beer or wine with each other. This custom was so ritualized that each particular group would have its own table – the stammtisch – reserved for it at the café or tavern. As men arrived, a place was made for them at their stammtisch, where the main activity was card playing. These male groups were completely integrated and Jewish men regularly met and played cards with Gentile friends. These friends were occasionally work mates or simply people one met at the same stammtisch. (Henry, 1984: 56).

My mother remembered her grandfather David participating on Saturday evenings during her summer visits. There were friendships between Jewish and German individuals and families that went beyond military service, ritualized card playing, fighting fires and buying and selling. Most of these probably ended after 1933 or earlier, when prohibitions on interaction with Jews went into place. But we learned of a few that survived bans on Jewish-German interaction. One of these was the friendship between my mother's uncle, Julius Rindsberg, and George Musgiller, a German man who lived in Dachsbach, about five miles to the south. Julius would travel through Dachsbach when he took cattle to market and Julius would stop and visit George. George helped Julius's cattle business by keeping an eye out in local barns for a good heifer Julius might make a profit from. Julius and his brother Felix and George had met while serving together in the army in the First World War and shared a common interest in horses. Years later, George's daughter remembered Julius as tall and slim, with a moustache and as a quiet, kind man. They called him 'der langer', the same nickname his father carried in Uehlfeld. By 1938, Julius was keeping his visits to after dark, sneaking in and out of the Musgiller house to protect his friend from arrest for being friendly with a Jew. Their friendship lasted until Julius never showed up again after November, 1938. We learned of Julius's friendship with George Musgiller in 1994 from George's grandson, Dr. Helmet Haberkamm, an English teacher and poet. Helmet had heard stories about Julius from his grandfather and mother and recalled that they always wondered what had happened to him after he stopped visiting. Helmet decided to find out, leading him to visit and correspond with my mother and me and other researchers. Helmet did find that Julius had moved to Frankfurt and then was killed at the Majdanek death camp in 1942. Helmet later visited the camp and found Julius's name on the memorial to victims at the camp. And we were able to fill out Julius's last years a bit more, learning that he had married in Frankfurt and lived there with his sister Gutta and her family.

But, it seems likely that such friendships were the exception, not the rule among Jews and Germans in rural Germany. My mother's and Walter Reed's experiences in Uehlfeld in the 1920s and early 1930s were that Jewish children played mainly with other Jewish children. In the cities, as discussed below, it was different in the early twentieth century with not only friendships but also many marriages among Jews and Germans, with Jewish men converting usually to Lutheranism.

8

City Life

As we have seen, over the closing decades of the nineteenth century Germany's Jewish population moved from small towns to larger towns and to the cities, with about 60 per cent of the population living in cities by 1900. Here we follow their path by moving our focus from Uehlfeld and other small towns to Frankfurt am Main, a major city where a Jewish community has existed from the twelfth century. As with rural life, the experiences of the Jewish communities across Germany's cities were not entirely uniform and differed in various ways from one another. Frankfurt serves a good example because its history exhibits some events and trends shared by other cities as well as some unique ones, and, also because it was the locale of a notable Jewish ghetto, a form of residential segregation and social isolation especially significant in the European Jewish experience.

In some general ways life for German Jews living in cities was not that different than life in small towns. There were years of acceptance and years of massacres, expulsions, and resettlement; residence was often possible only under the 'protection' of the rulers; high taxes were required; many worked as traders and money lenders; there was freedom to practice Judaism; and limited relations with Christian Germans. There were also some major differences. First, although Jews were often only a small percentage of a city's population, urban Jewish communities were considerably larger than those in towns. And with a larger population came socioeconomic differentiation and specialization with many more community institutions including synagogues, yeshivas, hospitals, voluntary associations and the accompanying religious specialists. Frankfurt, for example, in 1694 had eight rabbis, five cantors, two *shochetim,* and ten teachers serving a community of about 400 families. Second, although small town and city Jews made their livings in roughly the same occupations – trading, lending money, peddling, crafts, religious services – the wealth structure in cities was more complex with urban communities typically having a few very wealthy families (mainly the court Jews), those who made a comfortable living, those who lived at a subsistence level, and the poor. Third, while rural communities were largely recipients of externally-imposed change, Jewish urban communities generated change as the centres of Jewish learning and reforms, and also as the breeding ground for political unrest and agitation and for political reforms and emancipation.

The large, modern city of Frankfurt am Main – the financial capital of Europe – has a deep and significant history. It was a substantial settlement as early as the late 700s. Over the following centuries it emerged as an important commercial, transportation, and political centre under a mix of rulers including as a free imperial city of the Holy Roman Empire, several regional dynasties, Prussia, and since 1871 as the financial center of the newly-unified Germany. Frankfurt was a major centre of Jewish life, the locale of a large and notorious ghetto, the home to several prominent court Jews and its rabbis and scholars were leaders of both the Reform and Neo-Orthodoxy movements. It is easy today to find Frankfurt's Jewish heritage, unlike in Uehlfeld, as Frankfurt's is memorialised by more than fifty historical markers and monuments, the New Jewish Cemetery and the Jewish Museum.

Jews began coming to Frankfurt in the tenth century when they circulated in and out as traders at the city's popular trade fairs. The first known Jewish residents were traders from Worms who settled in Frankfurt in the twelfth century. From then on, except for several periods of expulsion, Jews lived and worked as traders, craftsmen, shop-keepers, and financers. They were massacred and fled when facing forced conversion in 1241 and then allowed to return in 1270. In 1349 they were massacred and fled again during the Plague persecutions, and returned again in 1360. They were massacred again in 1616 and 1624 but the community survived each time. As elsewhere, they lived under the protection of the emperor, a noblemen or the city council who in return for giving protection demanded the payment of heavy taxes and limited their civil and political rights. But they at times enjoyed certain privileges as traders and also because of the taxes they paid, they became key actors in the western European feudal economy, of which Frankfurt was a major centre. A Jewish community's influence on the rulers of small and large cities from the late sixteenth into the early nineteenth century was largely through its court Jews. Among the court Jews in Frankfurt were the Stern brothers, Low Deutz, Abraham Drach, Joseph Oppenheimer, and, most prominently, Mayer Amschel Rothchild, patriarch of the Rothchild banking family.

Other than their financial dealings with Germans, Frankfurt's Jews from 1462 to 1811 were socially, politically, and physically isolated, just as were Jews in many other European cities during the Middle Ages and the early modern period. As we saw, Jews in small towns often lived in their own neighborhood, although they were generally free to move about town and some Jews might even live outside the neighborhood. In some European cities and especially in southern Europe, even greater limits were placed on Jewish residential choices and travel, with Jews confined to ghettos; a legally delineated part of the city, often a single street, cordoned off from the city by a fence or wall, with locking gates at the ends of the street. The gates were locked from the outside at night and sometimes on Sundays and Christian holidays. They were also sometimes locked from the inside by the residents to keep out Christian rioters. Ghetto residence was another form of 'protection' and the Jewish residents paid heavy protection taxes. Some experts believe that the Jewish residents were not entirely displeased with the arrangement as the isolation and aggregation enabled the creation of vibrant Jewish communities and protected them from some assaults by Germans.

Ghettos as a means to contain and control a city's Jewish population emerged in southern Europe in the early Middle Ages. Although 'ghetto' has a broader meaning today, for European Jews it was the most extreme form of residential isolation. Ghettos were established at different times in different cities; the first in Spain, Portugal, and Italy perhaps as early as the eleventh century and later in Bohemia, Moravia, Austria, Hungary, Germany, Poland and Turkey. Major cities with ghettos included Madrid, Barcelona, Venice, Naples, Rome, Florence, Frankfurt, Mainz, Paris and Prague.

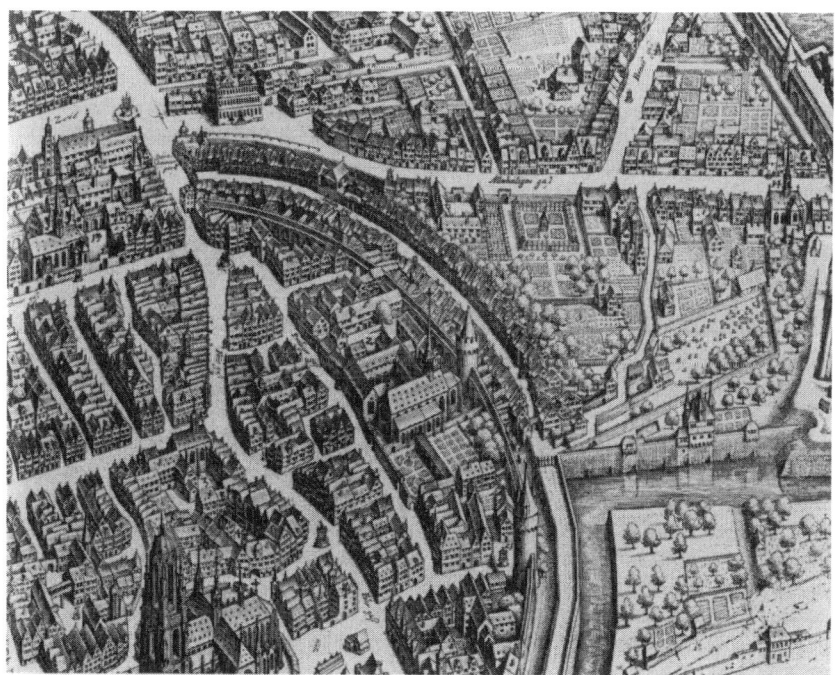

14. The Frankfurt ghetto in 1646, engraving by Matthäus Merian, Frankfurt.

Frankfurt's ghetto was established in 1462, to isolate and house the city's one hundred and fifty Jewish residents. As with many of the harsher persecutions of Jews, it was instigated by the church with the support of the government. Church officials wanted to move the few Jews living in Frankfurt away from the Catholic Church, distressed that Jews living there were able to witness Christians worshipping.

The Frankfurt ghetto has drawn considerable attention because it was founded relatively early, was very large, was a centre of Jewish life in Germany, and was especially horrible, at least according to outsiders. It was placed in the east end of Frankfurt, outside the city walls. Jews were not allowed to have shops outside the ghetto and were confined to the ghetto during non-business hours, behind the locked gates. Jews who did business in the city were able to conduct that business just outside the gates, as officials looked the other way, and some managed to circulate within the city. Some male ghetto residents were traders and moneylenders, some of whom traveled widely outside Frankfurt – as far as England – selling their wares and lending money on credit. Others such as labourers, bakers, butchers, shoemakers and tailors worked in the ghetto community. Over the centuries, many residents set up sewing shops in their homes, creating the basis for the textile industry which Jews came to dominate after emancipation.

As the Jewish population increased over the decades, the ghetto stretched longer and higher and eventually came to be regarded as the foulest ghetto in Europe. In 1610 it housed 3,000 men, women and children on a single street, about 320 yards long and 20 yards wide, lined by shops with apartments above them. As the wooden buildings rose higher and higher, the street below became darker, dirtier, the ghetto a fire trap and a petri dish for infectious disease. But the economic, physical and health limitations were balanced by intellectual and religious fluorescence as the community supported synagogues, schools, a community hall and hospital and became a centre of Jewish thought in Western Europe. Isolation in the ghetto did not guarantee full safety, with the ghetto raided by mobs in 1616 and again in 1624. In 1711 the ghetto burned down in an accidental fire but it was quickly rebuilt and about a third of the buildings went up in flames again ten years later and were again rebuilt. The ghetto was abolished by Napoleon in 1796 and in 1811 after Mayer Rothchild made a payment of 440,000 gulden to the city for the Jewish community, Jews were free to live outside it, although some chose to remain and were joined by Christian residents. The many Jewish institutions in the area kept the east end (*Ostend*) as the home of Frankfurt's Jewish community until some Jews began settling in the northwest district of the city in the middle of the nineteenth century.

The former ghetto remained a sign of separation and persecution but it disappeared over the years. The buildings were largely destroyed by a fire in the late 1800s. What was left of the old ghetto as well as newer buildings was reduced to rubble by British and American bombs during the Second World War. After the war, the area was cleared and reconstructed, removing all remains of the ghetto and reconfiguring the main street. All that is now visible of the ghetto are some building foundations and walls and artifacts that can be viewed at the Museum Judengasse.

The order in 1796 to open the ghetto was the first major sign of the future emancipation of Frankfurt's Jewish community. The community sought civil and political rights and civil reforms were achieved in 1811 with the opening of the ghetto following Rothchild's payment to the city. With the reorganization of Germany into thirty-nine states at the Congress of Vienna 1815 and Frankfurt classified as one of the four remaining free cities (with Hamburg, Bremen and Lubeck), emancipation was in the hands of the city government and they were hardly eager to proceed, revoking the civil rights granted just a few years earlier. In 1824 under pressure from Prussia whose emancipation law of 1812 had placed it with Austria in the forefront of the emancipation effort, civil rights were restored but restrictions on the number of Jewish marriages, some commercial activities, and holding political office remained in place. Full political rights were not granted until 1854 and then full equality in 1864, which remained in place after Frankfurt was incorporated into Prussia in 1866.

In addition to the opening of the ghetto, the Jewish community sought to expand its economic opportunities beyond trading and money lending, provide public education for its children, and the elite were much interested in social integration, which they hoped to realize through memberships in leading civic and fraternal organizations. The Frankfurt Jewish community was also receptive to religious reform and became a center of the Reform movement. By mid-century the community was religious diverse with adherents of several versions of Reform as well as Orthodoxy and neo-Orthodoxy, which now drew only a minority of Jewish Frankfurters.

Religious education had always been important, with the yeshiva in the ghetto providing religious education for boys from the late 1500s into the 1800s. Toward the end of the 1700s, as Enlightenment values took hold, Jewish parents sought public education for both their sons and daughters. Toward this end, early in the nineteenth century they began sending some of their children to Christian schools and then to the Philanthropin School founded by the Jewish community in 1804. The wealth-based structure of the ghetto lived on in the school with poorer children provided vocational training and wealthier children a public education with instruction in history, literature, German, Latin and mathematics. Over time the community moved away from vocational training and toward general education for all Jewish children and by 1895 we see the result with Jewish students constituting 15 per cent of the university student population across Germany.

Economic progress was slow in the first decades of emancipation as craft guilds especially resisted Jewish economic expansion and Germany remained a largely rural economy, providing less opportunity for expansion than other nations. The situation changed in the 1840s as industrialisation reached Germany and Frankfurt emerged as a major centre of commerce, finance and transportation. The Jewish experience as traders and money lenders and their literacy served them well in this new economic world and over the remainder of the century Jews across Germany entered the banking, accounting, insurance, legal, medical, transportation, catering, retail, and wholesale sectors and the professions in considerable numbers. By 1907, 64 per cent of employed Jewish men and 54 per cent of women worked in commerce. But, some occupations remained closed. Few Jewish scholars achieved the rank of full professor, few military officers made it beyond the lowest ranks, and Jews were rarely hired for civil service positions.

Social integration was more difficult and successful Jews (except for Mayer Rothchild) still found the doors closed to the Frankfurt's exclusive civic and fraternal organizations, whose members formed the city's influential business and political elite. The same was true for many of the city's numerous social, recreational and cultural organizations. Emancipation only went so far and the Jewish community reacted to these exclusions by forming its own clubs and societies, a trend that accelerated later in the Nazi period when the Jewish community was excluded from all but its own organizations. The community also continued to support its schools, hospital, and orphanage, with these open to all citizens.

9

City Life – Twentieth Century

As Germany entered the twentieth century, its Jewish population had been transformed from one that was mostly rural to one that was mostly urban, from one that was mostly poor to one that was mostly middle and upper-middle class, from one whose children received mainly a religious education to one whose children were among the highest university achievers, from one that was mostly traders and peddlers to one that was bankers, shopkeepers, lawyers, and physicians, and from one that was Orthodox to one that was mostly Reform.

My mother was born into this transformed world in Frankfurt on 31 October 1920. She spent the next eighteen years there until she fled to England on 23 July 1939. My mother's family roots in Frankfurt were not deep. Her father, Josef Gruenewald was born on 18 July 1889 in Heddernheim, then a small suburb, later incorporated into Frankfurt in 1910. Heddernheim's Jewish history is a familiar one. Jews established a *gemeinde* in Heddernheim in the sixteenth century. In 1545-47 there was a Jewish publishing house in town. Up until the mid-1800s most Jewish men were traders and then with emancipation came more occupational variety including craftsmen such as tailors and bookbinders. In 1815 the population was about 250 and it then grew to a high of 357 in 1850 before the usual out-migration made possible by emancipation led to a steady decline to 115 in 1871, 62 in 1905 and 32 in 1933. The community supported a synagogue, school, *mikvah* and cemetery, all destroyed in the Nazi era, with the cemetery now rebuilt.

My mother's mother, Rosa Rindsberg, came to Frankfurt from Uehlfeld as a teenager in about 1915 to work as a domestic for a Jewish family. She was making what was a common choice for young Jewish women from small towns; a city provided more opportunity than a small town. The post-emancipation rapid increase in the number of middle and upper-middle class Jewish homes created a demand for domestic servants. The demand was so great that the *Jüdischer Frauenbund* (JFB), the German-Jewish women's organization, established a programme to train and place these women in the homes of middle and upper-middle class Jewish families. The young women expected to benefit by learning skills such as sewing, cooking, housekeeping and child care, which would prepare them for marriage. Being in a city provided them access to other occupational choices and educational opportunities and also enabled them to meet men who might make suitable husbands. Rosa was one of several young Rindsberg women to move to a city. Several of her sisters and cousins in the extended Rindsberg clan also moved to cities like Frankfurt and Nuremberg and some trained at the Hotel Kronprinz (Crown Prince) which was established as a 'kosher' hotel in Wiesbaden in the 1890s by a sister of Rosa's father.

Josef and Rosa married in July 1920 and celebrated with a 'wedding trip' to Nuremberg. Josef was a butcher like his father. He served in the German army in the First World War and after returning home opened a butcher shop in Frankfurt, located at 23 Boernestrasse. The street had earlier been the centre of the ghetto. He expanded the business from retail to wholesale and sold both kosher and non-kosher meat. Over the years he moved the business several times and it was finally shut down in April 1933 when the tax authority deregulated his business as part of the Nazi boycott of Jewish businesses with all kosher butchers shut down across Germany. From then on Josef worked – often at night to escape Nazi detection – for non-Jewish butchers. The family lived in several apartments before settling at 40 Sandweg. The street was lined with four and five story apartment buildings, some with smaller residential buildings behind and with shops on the ground floors. Although not exclusively Jewish, Sandweg was home to several Jewish families and Jewish-owned shops. Lina Resch, a German woman who grew up on Sandweg, remembered neighbours who were an Orthodox rabbi, his wife and ten or eleven children. They were likely Eastern European Jews. They employed Lina who lived in the building behind theirs as a '*shabbos goy*' to tend the stove and perform other prohibited chores on Friday night and Saturday.

Born fifty years after emancipation, my mother and her generation as well as her parent's generation were German citizens with considerable opportunity in German society. Those opportunities were limited, as they were for all Germans, in some ways by Germany's difficult situation caused by its defeat in the First World War and the resulting financial crisis and then the Great Depression. But, being born a citizen meant that they saw themselves as German of the Jewish religion not as Jewish outsiders in Christian Germany. Being born and growing up in Frankfurt made a difference, too for, as discussed below, Frankfurt Jews saw themselves as different from other German Jews.

From the early twentieth century into the 1930s Frankfurt had a comparatively large Jewish population (about 5 per cent of the population as compared to less than 1 per cent for the whole of Germany and 4 per cent for Berlin), most of whom were assimilated into German society. Emancipation and the resulting educational and economic opportunities and religious reform had differentiated the Jewish community and there were now significant distinctions based on religious belief and practice (Reform versus Neo-Orthodox), wealth, occupation, neighbourhood of residence and even political beliefs (German loyalists v. Zionists).

Just as Frankfurt was a thriving city whose influence reached well beyond its walls, the Frankfurt Jewish community influenced Jewish and Christian life across Europe. The advice and money lent by families like the Rothchilds, Speyers and Oppenheimers influenced activity across the continent. A long succession of rabbis led and shaped the Orthodox, Neo-Orthodox and Reform Jewish movements and communities into the twentieth century. The community produced an equally long and influential list of scholars, writers, poets, musicians and politicians. Among those just in the modern era were the diarist Anne Frank, psychologist Erich Fromm, feminist Bertha Pappenheim, philosophers Martin Buber and Abraham Geiger, author Ludwig Börne, biologist Paul Erlich, economist Franz Oppenheimer and politicians Gabriel Riesser and Ludwig Landmann (Frankfurt's Lord Mayor from 1924 to 1933).

By the opening of the twentieth century, the Jewish communities in Germany's cities had become for the most part what sociologists call an 'invisible minority', meaning that Jewish individuals looked like the general German population in dress, language and behaviour, which made them not readily identifiable as Jewish. Some urban Jews were also invisible because they were no longer Jews. By the 1930s about 25 per cent of Jews (mainly men in cities) had either rejected Judaism for philosophical, religious or lifestyle reasons and practiced no religion or had converted usually to Lutheranism and some then married Christian women, raising their children as Christians. What was most visible where the Jewish community's institutions – synagogues, cemeteries, schools, orphanages and hospitals, although they were relatively few in number and except for the synagogues often were open to both Christians and Jews. But, while individual Jews did not stand out from the general population, the Jewish community across Germany did continue to stand out, especially in the minds, speeches and writings of those who continued to object to the growing Jewish wealth and what they saw as undue influence in Germany society. Jewish achievements and involvement in German society were hard to miss as Jewish men and women were at the forefront of journalism, science, medicine, law, banking, manufacturing, the retail sector and arts and literature.

Jews were invisible not just because they looked, spoke and acted German, but also as always there were few to be seen, as Jews remained only a small percentage of the German population and there were still many communities with no Jews at all. The Jewish population of Germany was 615,021 in 1910. By 1933 it had decreased to 525, 000, leaving Jews as a small minority, only .76 per cent of the national population. This rapid decrease in the Jewish population in the early 1900s was the inevitable result of a low Jewish birth rate combined with the Jewish emigration discussed previously. Frankfurt with 26,158 Jews had the second largest Jewish population of German cities, although it was dwarfed by the 144,000 Jews who lived in Berlin, the national capital. The pre-War population of other German cities was also relatively small: Breslau (20,000), Hamburg (17,000), Hanover (13,000), Leipzig (12,000), Danzig (10,000), Munich (9,500) and Nuremberg (9, 000).

Frankfurt was a demographic exception not just because of it relatively large Jewish population but also because the population remained stable between 1910 and 1933, as the Jewish population decreased elsewhere. This stability resulted from the large number of Jews moving to the city from rural areas including the several Rindsberg women which offset the outmigration of Jews who left Frankfurt. From about 1923 onwards Frankfurt was a haven for Jews fleeing Nazi persecutions in small towns in western and southern Germany. In the 1930s, with families and children leaving the country for the United States, South America and Western Europe, and with many older people moving in from the rural areas, Germany's Jewish population began to be transformed into a population that was mainly middle-aged or elderly. It became older over the decade as Jewish children and young people like my mother and her friends and cousins fled to the U.S., England, Palestine and elsewhere. By 1939, 82 per cent of Jewish children under fifteen and 83 per cent of young adults aged 16-24 had left Germany. In Frankfurt and across Germany the Jewish community was now not just mainly middle aged and elderly but with many men imprisoned, mainly female.

Frankfurt's Jewish community's upward social and economic mobility and intellectual achievement over the nineteenth century and into the twentieth emerged in the context of Frankfurt's position as Europe's financial centre. That context had a profound impact on the community's cultural identity as well as on the self-image of Jews who lived there. Many of those who were born and grew up there – if not most – felt culturally German and believed that they were full members of German society, which by law they were, until the Nuremberg Laws of 1935. They also had a strong allegiance to and identification with Frankfurt, seeing themselves as 'Frankfurt Jews'. This self-image came to distinguish them – favourably in their own view and less favourably in the view of other German Jews – from Jews elsewhere in Germany and especially in Berlin. Jewish Frankfurters saw themselves as intellectual, at the cutting edge of Jewish thought and reform, modern, urbane and sophisticated.

This self-image of the 'Frankfurt Jew' was carried to new homes by many who fled Frankfurt in the 1930s. Many Frankfurt refugees settled in the Washington Heights neighbourhood on the upper west side of Manhattan. There they developed a thriving community that retained many of Frankfurt's German and Jewish institutions and customs, the most obvious being the continued use of German as their daily language. The community became known as Frankfurt on the Hudson. The same was true among those who fled to London. They settled mainly in the northwest district, founded their own Reform synagogue and employed rabbis who had emigrated from Germany.

As we saw, my mother's parents were recent arrivals in Frankfurt and were not part of the economic or intellectual elite. In fact, it seems that few Rindsbergs or Gruenewalds took advantage of the educational and employment opportunities that produced the large Jewish middle and upper-middle classes in early twentieth century Germany. Regardless of their economic mobility or lack thereof, my mother like others of her age who were born there saw themselves as Frankfurters who were German citizens and adherents of Judaism, with no contradiction between these two identities. This was a major departure from the past when being Jewish meant one could not also be German. There were no efforts to convert Jews to Christianity (although some converted for marriage or other reasons) and Jewish students in public school were given books about Judaism, written in German, to cover the religion requirement of the curriculum. For urban Jewish children there was little to distinguish them from German children other than they went to church on Sunday and if Jewish children went at all, it was on Saturday. Many Jewish children, like my mother, had Christian friends, although many of those friendships, although not all, ended when the Nazis came to power and restricted contact with Jews.

Jewish assimilation was more rapid and fuller in the cities. Nonetheless, they continued to face some restrictions such as employment in the civil service, or rising high in the officer ranks of the military and were the object of anti-Jewish speeches and writings following emancipation, motivated by a desire to limit or end Jewish progress and influence. What struck me as a remarkably clear understanding of the Jewish position in German society was revealed in a letter written in April, 1941 by my mother's Frankfurt friend Ilse Fuchs (now safe in Chicago) in which she commented at length about what she correctly expected would be the fate of the families they had left behind in Frankfurt. In explaining why she thought older people had chosen not to flee Germany, she perceptively noted that that they were not 'what they believed they were'. She meant that they had believed that they were German but that they were not, because some Germans or perhaps many Germans had never accepted them as German.

We have seen how education was a driving concern during the emancipation process and it gained even more importance in urban Jewish communities following emancipation. Jewish students attended public schools or private Jewish schools and some were taught by private tutors. A significant percentage, and a much larger percentage then in the German population, went on to university, especially before 1920 when the Germans began to catch up. There was some variation across Germany in how Jews children were educated – in Berlin most went to public schools, in Frankfurt most went to private schools, the Philanthropin School being the most prestigious. The interest in vocational training in the early years of the emancipation process had faded quickly and one hundred years later in the early twentieth century few Jewish adolescents attended vocational schools, preferring instead a general education. Formal religious instruction came in the public school and in religious school, if parents so chose to send their children. Jewish identity and friendships were forged through membership in the *Bund*, the vernacular name for the Jewish youth group, as well as Jewish sports and literary and arts societies, although many Jewish children also had Christian friends.

Although it is convenient to speak of the Jewish community in Frankfurt or other cities as if it were one, in reality the near equality and success the Jewish community achieved over the last half of the nineteenth century produced very clear divisions in the Jewish community in Frankfurt and other cities by the twentieth. A new class hierarchy based on a combination of wealth, religion and geography had emerged. Working-class and middle class Jews who adhered to Reform or Orthodox Judaism, although in the revived Neo-Orthodox form that emerged in the 1850s, lived mainly in the east end of Frankfurt, near what had been the ghetto. Several Jewish institutions – synagogues, schools, clubs and societies, and a hospital were located in this neighbourhood. Wealthier Jews who adhered to Reform Judaism lived mainly in the northwest district and supported two synagogues and schools there. Many Jews in Frankfurt were upper-middle class lawyers, physicians, bankers and owners of retail and manufacturing firms.

The Neo-Orthodox and Reform communities in Frankfurt were represented by separate religious *gemeinde* which sometimes battled for control of the Jewish institutions. In addition to these two main Jewish religious communities, a small number were drawn to Zionism, whose ideology and political activism marked their identity. All three communities supported various service, civic, athletic and youth organizations and there were also some of these organizations not affiliated with any particular religious orientation. In all, in the 1920s there were about thirty Jewish voluntary organizations in the city, not including the synagogues, schools, and service organizations.

A fourth group in the mix of Jews in Frankfurt and other cities in the early twentieth century were the *Ostjuden*. Over 100,000 Eastern European Jews (mainly from Poland and Russia) had come to Germany as refugees from the *pogroms* that began in 1880. The German government considered them undesirable, claiming that they did not fit in and took jobs and housing needed by Germans. After the First World War 40,000 were deported or forced to leave Germany. The Jewish community did not know quite what to do with these foreigners. Certainly they were Jews but not German Jews nor Frankfurt Jews. They looked and spoke and behaved like the anti-Semitic stereotype of 'The Jew' that the now assimilated German-Jewish community wished was a forgotten embarrassment of the past. Many German Jews worried that these Jewish foreigners would stir up further anti-Semitism. These Eastern European Jewish men were hardly invisible, standing out with their rough, heavy coats, covered heads and long beards. They were poor,

15. The Boernplatz Synagogue in Frankfurt, c. 1930, eight years before its destruction.

uneducated, devout Orthodox and worshipped in their own synagogues. They spoke Eastern European Yiddish, not German.

The cultural disconnect between wealthier Frankfurt Jews and the *Ostjuden* and the Zionists was on the mind of Otto Frank, the father of Anne Frank, when he was considering moving the family to Palestine in the early 1930s, before the Franks moved to Switzerland and then Amsterdam:

> We don't belong there. We Jews have lived in Germany for almost two thousand years. We are educated, cultured, we are Jewish of course but not Orthodox. We have nothing in common with those eastern Jews, the merchants and factory workers who are largely Zionists because they have no other choice. We have absolutely nothing to do with those Eastern European rabbis. No, we could live in another European country, or America, but not in Asia [Palestine]. (Pressler, 2011: 35)

The Jewish community supported the *Ostjuden* but also sought to assimilate them as quickly as possible by providing education and social services and jobs. The *Jüdischer Frauenbund* (JFB), as it did with rural German Jewish women, also trained and placed some of these young women as domestics with Jewish families.

Thus, the social, economic, and religious variation which characterised the Jewish experience in Germany in the first decades of the twentieth century made the Jewish experience far more complicated and much different than previously. Many Jews now defined themselves as German first and Jewish second, despite continuing social segregation, exclusion from certain occupations and a Germany minority who still considered Jews to be outsiders with too much wealth and influence on German life. In very general terms, this was the status of the Jewish community in 1933. Although our focus has been on the Jewish experience before the Holocaust, no book about the Jewish German experience is complete without coverage of that period, usually defined as from January 1933 to May 1945, and we now turn to the Holocaust experience in Germany.

10
The Holocaust and New Communities

'What did I do to deserve all this? Why do they hate us, we didn't harm anybody, did we?' George Musgiller remembered his friend, Julius Rindsberg, asking him these questions in 1938. Julius's Uehlfeld was a hotbed of Nazi activity. Since the early 1920s Julius witnessed and had been the target of regular persecution, meant to drive him and the town's several dozen remaining Jewish residents from their homes. As he rode his horse through the town gatehouse he couldn't miss the sign warning Jews out of Uehlfeld just as he couldn't miss the 'hanging' Jew in front of the church just around the corner from his home. He knew it was conspicuously hung to make him feel unwelcome, to scare him into moving away. Knowing something about Julius's life, we can understand his anguished plea for answers. The persecutions made no sense to him. He had done nothing to harm Germany nor his German neighbours. He was born a German citizen, fought for his homeland in the First World War along with brothers Felix and Ludwig, and earned a modest living as a cattle dealer, remaining in town to take over his father's business as Jewish sons had done for generations. George had no comforting response to his friend's plea, but defying the law and putting himself and his family at risk, he remained friends with Julius and welcomed him into his home until November 1938, until Julius came no more, having been finally run out of town just before *Kristallnacht*.

For obvious and good reason the Holocaust is the best-described, most-discussed and most controversial period in Jewish German history. It is also the period that is remembered by numerous monuments to the Jewish community, to individual communities, to Jewish institutions and to individual Jewish victims. Thus, there seems no need to review here even the basics of the Holocaust as that information is so readily available. Rather, in sticking with the aim of this volume, it seems more worthwhile to keep the focus on Jewish Germany and outline how the German Holocaust experience differed from that experience in other nations.

There were several fundamental differences. First, the Holocaust began in Germany and its methods and goals were brought from there by Germans to annihilate the Jewish populations of other nations conquered by Germany. Because it began in Germany, the Holocaust began earlier there, not in the

16. The first Holocaust memorial in Frankfurt, erected in 1965. The names of some Nazi-established ghettos, concentration camps and extermination centres appear around the base.

'official' year of 1933 when Hitler took power and persecution of Jews and others became government policy, but in the early 1920s in some regions as the National Socialist German Workers' Party (Nazi Party or NSDAP) came to power, with removal of Jews from Germany a central element of its agenda.

A second key difference is that far fewer German Jews, both in actual numbers and as a percentage of the nation's Jewish population in 1933, died during the Holocaust than did the Jews of several other nations. In 1933 about 525,000 Jews lived in Germany. About 50 per cent were killed between 1942 and 1945. This was considerably fewer than killed in the eastern European nations of Poland, eastern Russia, Lithuania, Ukraine, Hungary and Czechoslovakia although more than in western European nations such as France, Belgium and Italy. To some extent the difference in number of victims is due simply to the different sizes of the Jewish populations. Poland had the most victims because at over three million it had the largest Jewish population. But, the variation in number of victims was also due to the relative freedom of the Jewish populations to flee to safer places before the deportations and killings began. This was mostly impossible in Eastern Europe after those nations came under German rule and even before, but possible in Germany and Western Europe until late in 1941.

Of the about 525,000 Jews in Germany in 1933 about 400,000 were German-born and German citizens. The others were mainly Eastern European Jews (mostly Polish) who had been born in Germany but were not citizens. By October 1941 when Jewish emigration was banned, some 160,000 to 180,000 Jews remained in Germany. The approximately 350,000 who escaped found safety in neighbouring nations (France, Switzerland, Belgium, Denmark, the Netherlands) and farther away in the United States, Palestine, Britain, South America, China (Shanghai) and elsewhere. Some of those who went to neighbouring nations found only short-term safety there, as many were rounded up, deported to death camps in the east and killed after Germany conquered those nations in 1940 and initiated the Final Solution in 1941.

For the Nazi government, obsessed with the Jewish Question, a more basic question than the number of Jews was the complicated question of just who was to be classified as a Jew in Germany, and later in conquered nations as well. As we saw in Frankfurt, the assimilation that took place over the sixty or so years following emancipation produced a complex Jewish population including those of various degrees of Jewish ancestry, those who had converted to Christianity, and those who had been born Jewish but as adults chose to reject religion and saw themselves as neither Jewish nor Christian. The Nuremberg Laws of 1935 tried to deal with this issue by classifying the German population into three categories: (1) Germans (Aryans), (2) Jews, and (3) *mischelenge*, literally people of 'mixed-blood', Jewish and Aryan, although the term was meant as derogatory as in 'mongrel' or 'half-breed'. Jews were defined as individuals with three or four Jewish grandparents. *Mischlenge* were further classified as either first or second degree. First degree *mischlenge* were individuals with two Jewish grandparents. They were classified as Jewish if they were also a member of the Jewish community or were married to a Jew on 14 November 1935 or after, or his or her parents were married after 17 November 1935 and one parent was Jewish, or was born out of wedlock after 31 July 1936 and one parent was married. Second degree *mischlenge* were individuals with just one Jewish grandparent. In 1939 the government listed 72,000 individuals as first degree and 39,000 as second degree. In addition there were several hundred other Germans who had less degrees of Jewish ancestry and an unknown number – probably over 100,000 – who successfully concealed their Jewish ancestry.

Beyond classifying people, the *mischlenge* question also concerned what to do with people so classified. Second degree individuals faced employment restrictions and were banned from marrying Germans but were not imprisoned. During the Final Solution discussions in 1942 proposals were made to deport and execute or sterilize *mischelenge*, but the proposals were never converted into policy. To some extent, how individual *mischleng* were treated depended less on the official classification and more on an individual's occupation and his or her value to Germany, his or her political connections, and the attitude of local Nazi officials charged with enforcing government policy.

We can return to my mother's family and Uehlfeld for an example of how this issue of Jewish identity played out in some families. After *Kristallnacht* in November 1938, three individuals known to be of Jewish ancestry still lived in the town – Elsa Rindsberg Kestler and her son Walter and daughter Bertha. Elsa, my mother's mother's first cousin, had been married for twenty-five years to German farmer and shopkeeper Fritz Kestler. Elsa had converted to Lutheranism and the children were so raised. Harassed by local Nazis, Elsa was actually not in Uehlfeld that November, having fled Nazi persecution in the town earlier in the year to live with relatives in Nuremburg, leaving Fritz and the children behind. Fritz applied for a residence permit for Elsa from the NSDAP office in Neustadt. The response was not encouraging:

> Regarding your request for a residence permit for your wife, I have to inform you of the following. Your wife, born Elsa Rindeberg [sic], is a full-blooded Jewess. That is why she has repeatedly shown to all members of her race, through personal contact and all possible help, that she belongs to them. She has given shelter to Jews who felt

threatened. I am not astonished that you were not enough of a man to put an end to this, since someone who admits that he has been happily married to a Jewess for 25 years shows that he is badly contaminated by this evil Jewish spirit. If, at the time, you were oblivious enough of your race to marry a Jewess against the warnings of your parents, you cannot expect today that an exception be made for your Jewish wife (to be allowed to return to her family) (Lefkovitz, 2013: 11)

Elsa did return to Uehlfeld and spent the war there, evidently able to now do so because, according to the family story, Fritz had a relative active in the NSDAP who intervened on her behalf although it is more likely that she was allowed to live in town because they married before 1935 and under German law were considered to be in a 'privileged mixed-marriage'.

Son Walter, classified as a *mischleng* of the first degree, with his two Jewish grandparents, was engaged to a Christian woman. The engagement was terminated as the marriage was prohibited by Nazi miscegenation laws. Walter's Jewish heritage barred him from military service and instead he was drafted into the Reichsarbeitsdienst (RAD), a labour organization, which provided support services for the Wehrmacht during the war. Years later he said that being of half-Jewish ancestry probably saved his life as it limited his service to the rear-guard RAD. He returned to town after the war, married and the couple had two daughters, who still live in the area. A prominent citizen, he served as the chief of the volunteer fire department from 1961 to 1971 and was made honorary chief after his retirement. His sister, Bertha Kestler, also remained in town after the war as did Fritz and Elsa.

Leaving their nation and escaping death was an option few Jews had in the conquered nations. When the NSDAP came to power in Germany in January, 1933 most – perhaps all Jews – knew from their experiences of the previous ten years or so that Nazi rule would bring more trouble and their full legal and near actual equality was threatened and sure to come to an end. About 37,000 fled that year. They were mainly those who openly opposed the NSDAP (Socialists and Communists), those who had their business shut down, and government officials who lost their jobs. Many were wealthy, or had political or family connections outside Germany, or had professions or skills desired in other nations. Those who did not have these immediate needs to leave or the advantages that enabled a quick exit remained in Germany, hoping that Nazi persecution would not become too oppressive and as the persecution intensified hoping that the Nazi's would soon lose power. From what we now know about the fate of those Jews who stayed behind, it does seems like foolish and wishful thinking. But, in the context of the times – Nazi Germany in the mid-1930s – it may have been unrealistic but not totally foolish. Despite the relentless propagandizing of the 'charismatic Führer' and Hitler's economic reforms and military and infrastructure building, there was significant discontent with his rule, especially among the German working class which benefited little from his initiatives. Additionally, the harshness of the persecution of Jews waxed and waned from 1934 to 1938 and varied in intensity and effect from district to district and even within towns and cities within districts. In Middle Franconia, for example, despite it being a hotbed of Nazi support, resistance by German farmers to ending their economic relationships with Jewish cattle dealers allowed some of those dealers to stay in business for an additional two or three years. Accompanying discontent and the occasional lessening of persecution was the hope that the regime would fall from power, although people also realized that there was no viable alternative. These factors plus the unwillingness of other nations to take Jewish refugees meant that from 1934 through 1937 less than 25,000 Jews were able to leave Germany each year.

The Nazi government did encourage Jews to leave into 1941, although immigration taxes, confiscation of Jewish property, and limits on how much money could be taken with them did not make it easy. But the real problem was where to go, as other nations made it difficult to find refuge within their borders.

There is a dark joke about Jews in Nazi Germany: the pessimists went to New York; the optimists to Auschwitz. The first part is true in general terms as those who could did flee to many places, but the second part, not so much. Those who stayed were not optimistic, many stayed because of the cruel reality that they had nowhere to go. Jews, or large numbers of Jews, were not welcome in most other nations. Nearly all nations had highly restrictive immigration policies based on their national interests and most governments saw accepting German Jewish refugees in the 1930s as antagonistic to those interests. The 1930s was the decade of the Great Depression and government budgets were stretched trying to provide jobs and housing and support for their own citizens. Refugees, let alone Jewish refugees, were seen as a drain in good times; in bad, an obstacle in the path of economic recovery. In an all-too familiar argument against immigration, governments routinely claimed that allowing in large numbers of Jewish refugees would put a drain on government services, would require the government to support some of them, and the refugees would take jobs and housing needed by their own citizens. In addition, although it was less often mentioned publicly, many believed that the German Jews would not fit in. All of these claims are, of course, ones immigrants have heard over and over again throughout human history, including around the world today. Just how unwilling the world community was to accept Jewish refugees from Germany and Austria became fully clear at the July 1938 Evian Conference in France, convened by U.S. President Franklin Delano Roosevelt to address the Jewish refugee crisis. Of the thirty-two nations participating only the Dominican Republic agreed to accept more Jewish refugees. Resistance was so strong that a year later the U.S. Congress refused to pass legislation that would have allowed 20,000 Jewish children to enter the country. Clearly, anti-Semitism in the State Department played a role in shaping U.S. policy and most everywhere else except in Palestine.

Several other practicalities also kept Jews in Germany. First, as we have seen, most Jews in Germany were German citizens (until 1935), were assimilated into German life, and defined themselves as German nationals. Their national self-identification as Germans was little different than that of people of Jewish or Italian or African ancestry in the United States today who see themselves as Americans. Practical consideration mattered as well. Leaving Germany meant departing their homeland and starting a new life somewhere else, a daunting task for older people with little money or marketable skills. Working-class and middle-class families were not wealthy and most people did not have the education or skills that would have made it easy or even possible to start over elsewhere. Parents worried that in a new land they would be a burden on their children. Those who did leave often had to take work far beneath their abilities and skills. For example, some 25,000 women were admitted into Great Britain in the late 1930s when they agreed to work only as domestic servants for British middle-class families. Many of these women were middle or upper middle class themselves and had employed domestic servants in their homes in Germany, making for an often difficult role reversal for them in Great Britain. Another reality keeping some in Germany was that leaving often meant that families would be torn apart, with some left behind or parents and children fleeing to different nations. This was a wrenching decision for parents, who usually chose to stay behind themselves, sending their children off to England on the *Kindertransport* or elsewhere and hoping to reconnect later. A third consideration was the history of the Jewish experience in Germany. Parents and grandparents knew the history of persecutions, mass killings and expulsions that had occurred over the centuries. But they also knew that these all eventually passed and that Jews then returned to their normal though restricted lives. They were hardly optimistic, but some hoped, unrealistically we now know, that this history would repeat itself.

Returning to the emergence of the Holocaust on Germany, it is worth exploring its appearance in Bavaria, Franconia, and Uehlfeld, a state, district, and town where the NSDAP drew early and enthusiastic support in the early 1920s and then spread north across Germany from its breeding ground in Munich and propaganda center in Nuremberg. Ridding Germany of its Jewish citizens was a central goal of the Party, following the directive of its leader, Adolf Hitler, set forth in his agenda for a restoration of Germany's greatness in his *Mein Kampf*. Many small-town Franconians were drawn to the Party's German nationalism and anti-Semitism and some men in many small, mainly Protestant towns like Uehlfeld were among its loudest and nastiest backers. These early devotees were often small-scale businessmen, their employees and civil servants. Farmers were slower to sign on, probably because they still relied on Jewish traders to sell their products and lend them money. Initially, the NSDAP had far less appeal outside Bavaria and performed poorly in early elections. The Party captured less than 3 per cent of the vote in the 1928 federal election (it had taken 6.5 per cent and 3 per cent in the two 1924 elections). But its electoral support was double that in Bavaria, at 6 per cent of the vote, with its strongest turnout in Franconia. In the Neustadt district which included Uehlfeld, the Party's candidates took the most votes; 30 per cent of Uehlfelders voted for Party candidates, ten times the 3 per cent national level of support. The official party newspaper, the *Völkischer Beobachter*, told its readers of the crucial role played by small towns like Uehlfeld:

> Bavaria, in which the national Socialist vote was 6 per cent of all the votes cast, marches at the lead of the Reich In small towns and villages National Socialist mass meetings with good speakers are events and are often talked about for weeks on end... (Mühlberger, 2004: 296)

With preservation of the 'Aryan race' and anti-Semitism a central element of the Nazi platform in Bavaria, Jews became an early target for their Nazi neighbours. The harshness of Jewish persecution varied across the region, with persecution led by local Nazis especially harsh in Middle Franconia. Several factors coalesced to make Middle Franconia especially receptive to Nazi anti-Semitic ideology. One was that the region had a long history of anti-Jewish sentiment and assaults, linked as we have seen to the anti-Semitic agenda of the Lutheran Church, carried out by its local pastors. Middle Franconia was mostly Lutheran while most of Bavaria's other administrative districts were mostly Catholic. Make no mistake, the Catholic Church was hardly tolerant, but in the Nazi era was more sympathetic to Jews and resistant to Nazi persecution. A second factor was that Middle Franconia had a relatively large Jewish population, at 1.12 per cent (11,621 in 1933) the largest of all Bavarian districts, and twice the percentage of the entire Jewish

Bavarian population. Finally, Middle Franconia had the misfortune of including Nuremberg, the centre of Nazi propaganda and was placed in the NSDAP administrative district overseen by virulent anti-Semite and leading propagandist Julius Streicher (1885-1946), the publisher of the *Der Stürmer* newspaper, a leading Nazi propaganda vehicle. It was Streicher's anti-Semitic tirades that Uehlfeld Jews and their neighbours heard on their radios and read in his newspaper and those who survived would be repelled by the hatred for the rest of their lives. Streicher was convicted of crimes against humanity by the International Military Tribunal at Nuremberg in 1946 and hanged. Jews were not just an early target, but also an easy one as in rural communities because they were few in number, isolated from Jewish or other organizations that might assist them, and known to be Jewish. In Frankfurt and other cities Jews, young people – especially young women – could 'pass' as German in public, an impossibility in small towns.

Uehlfeld men were among the first to form a local NDSAP branch in 1923, ten years before Hitler came to power, and attacks on the Jewish residents were reported as early as 1921 and certainly were underway by 1923. The NSDAP moved quickly to make all cities and towns *Judenfrei*. Harassment of Jewish Uehlfelders at first included verbal insults, window breaking, economic boycotts, and restrictions on interaction with non-Jews with the goal of what today would be called ethnic cleansing. In addition to finally solving the 'Jewish Question' the Nazis and their local supporters realized that they would benefit materially from the Jewish exodus as they could purchase at deep discounts Jewish property or simply take it after the Jewish owners fled. But not all of their German neighbours supported the Nazi agenda and some ignored the Nazi orders and defended and assisted Jews. Fred Fields (b. Siegfried Dingfelder), who was born in Uehlfeld and left in 1931, remembered one telling incident:

> I remember one man got up and made a speech in a beer garden where everybody met. He said, 'I don't understand what they want from the Jews here, they're never done us any harm. They're just like we are.' The next day he disappeared and ended up in a concentration camp. He came back six weeks later and never spoke another word about it. He was cured.

When the Nazis came to power in January, 1933 attacks on Jews escalated. Hitler's first priority was silencing his socialist and communist political opponents, some 10,000 of whom he imprisoned or had killed. He then turned his attention to the Roma (Gypsies) and resolving the Jewish Question, enacting laws designed to drive Jews from Germany. In many towns, signs were posted telling Jews to get out or stay out of town. In Uehlfeld, wooden signs on the roads into town and on the gatehouse expressed that wish of at least a substantial minority of Uehlfelders.

A gallows was erected in front of the church with a 'Jewish' effigy swinging from its noose. Ironically, adjacent to the hanging Jew was the town's war memorial which listed town men killed in the First World War including two Jewish soldiers. Jews were banned from swimming in the Aisch, and then banned from walking on the town's sidewalks and assaulted on the streets. In 1935 gravestones were overturned and later stones were broken and some hauled off and piled along a wall, waiting to be removed and destroyed or re-cycled as building or road material. In 1936 Nazis marched through town smashing the windows of Jewish homes and the synagogue and in 1938 two Jews were arrested for 'treasonable utterances'. On 20 October 1938 a local Nazi leader and 20 followers again marched through town, again breaking windows on Jewish homes.

The assaults and economic restrictions drove out most of the few dozen Jews left in Uehlfeld. On 24 October 1938 the Nazi Nuremberg newspaper *Fraenkische Tageszeitung* listed Uehlfeld in its front-page column where it regularly boasted of German towns that were now *Judenfrei*. This claim was premature, but only by a few weeks. After the 20 October attack, Jewish families were given three-day's notice to leave town. Still, fifteen or so Jewish residents remained in town and did not leave until 9 November when the NSDAP office in Neustadt gave them twenty-four hours to pack what they could and depart.

Not surprisingly, given the early, large, and dedicated NSDAP following in the region, Jews and Jewish communities in Middle Franconia suffered badly on *Kristallnacht*. At least 42 synagogues, 115 shops or business and 594 homes were damaged or destroyed. In Uehlfeld, the synagogue was burned, with only the outside walls left standing. Adjacent Jewish homes which were now empty of their Jewish owners and the former Jewish school were left undamaged. The burning of the synagogue served no practical purpose as the few Jews in town were no longer using the building and had offered to sell it.

By the late 1930s, this was no longer something of harsh outlier, but typical of what Jews were experiencing across Germany. When the war ended in May 1945, the Holocaust had destroyed Germany's Jewish communities, obliterated their pasts, and killed about half of the German Jewish population. About 265,000 Jewish Germans survived; some 250,000 safely in other nations (mainly Israel, the United States and Great Britain); about 15,000 in concentration, death and labour camps; and some 2,000 in Germany itself. The end of the war brought an influx of Jewish refugees and displaced persons – as many as 250,000 – into Germany, Austria and Italy where they were sheltered in refugee centres and displaced person camps administered by the United Nations and the Allied forces. Most came from Poland, Lithuania, Russia, Romania and Czechoslovakia and what to do with them quickly became a contentious political issue both within and outside the Jewish community. Some officials wanted to send them back to their nations of origin, but most refugees refused, arguing correctly that they would face persecution there at the hands of their Christian former co-nationalists who had aided the German occupiers. Most preferred to move on to Palestine or the United States. The British prohibited settlement in Palestine but between 1945 and 1948 about 100,000 made it there anyway, often following a circuitous route going north into Denmark first than to southern Europe or Cyprus and finally to Palestine. In 1948 centres cleared out as the situation improved with the founding of the State of Israel and reforms in American immigration policy which allowed in up to 200,000 refugees.

By 1950 Germany's Jewish population had declined to about 15,000: 6,000 refugees from Eastern Europe who chose to stay in Germany, 6,000 Jewish Germans survivors who returned to Germany after the war, and 2,000 from other nations who moved to Germany. Very few Jewish German survivors were interested in returning to Germany and even if they had wanted to return, mass return would have been impossible as the new German government, international aid organizations and Jewish organizations all opposed their return. The 6,000 or so who did return after the war were a unique group. Most had been opponents of the Nazi regime (Communists and Socialists) who returned to continue the fight against fascism. They were secular Jews who viewed themselves as political activists, not Jews.

Germany's departed Jewish communities were largely forgotten after the war. There were the more immediate issues of settling refugees from the east and founding the State of Israel for the Jewish organizations outside Germany and the few German Jews in Germany had neither the interest nor resources to pursue the past. As for the Germans, their nation's Nazi past and the fate of their Jewish neighbours were of little interest and hardly as important as rebuilding their own lives and communities. One exception was the Jewish cemeteries which had been vandalized and destroyed across Germany. In accord with the Jewish religious requirement to maintain cemeteries and the reality that there were no longer Jews in Germany to maintain the cemeteries, the German nation and states took responsibility for reconstruction and care. But, interest in the Jewish past emerged only years later in the 1990s as part of the broader interest in Jewish history across Germany.

17. The Westend Synagogue in Frankfurt in 1992, the only one in the city to survive *Kristallnacht*.

It seems fitting to close by taking the narrative full circle with a brief look at Germany's Jewish communities today. As in the past, there is no single community. We see in Germany today three Jewish communities. First, the communities of the past, remembered and memorialised by hundreds of historic markers and restored cemeteries, Holocaust memorials, museums, educational materials, heritage tours, and tens of thousands of *stolpersteine* – memorial stones placed in sidewalks for those killed in the Holocaust – in over 600 German communities. Second, the actual Jewish community living in Germany which in 2016 numbered about 120,000 individuals (although some believe it may be twice that size), most of Eastern European ancestry whose ancestors came to Germany following the SecondWorld War and especially in the 1990s from Russia. Third, some 200,000 Jews who are naturalised German citizens but hold dual citizenship in other nations of their birth and, except for about 15,000 individuals who have actually relocated continue to live in their home nations, have never lived in Germany, and probably never will. Most of these non-resident 'Jewish Germans' are children and grandchildren of Holocaust victims and survivors who under Germany's 1948 constitution as descendants of victims and survivors were given the right to claim German citizenship:

> Former German citizens who between January 30, 1933 and May 8, 1945 were deprived of their citizenship on political, racial, or religious grounds, and their descendants, shall on application have their citizenship restored. They shall be deemed never to have been deprived of their citizenship if they have established their domicile in Germany after May 8, 1945 and have not expressed a contrary intention.

Most of these individuals live in Israel and the United States with growing number in Great Britain. In some ways they represent an odd bridge between the past and present. Their citizenship is based on family ties to the now-gone Jewish German communities of the past, with many tracing their Jewish German ancestry back centuries. But, their desire for German citizenship is driven largely by current political and economic uncertainty in their own nations as well as educational, employment and travel opportunities provided by Germany's membership in the European Union. But, in a repeat of one of the patterns of the Jewish past in Germany, they have come to see the Germany of 2017 as a nation of growing uncertainty as regards the safety and future opportunity for Jewish citizens. They read and hear about growing anti-Semitism (despite the tiny Jewish population), associated with the both the nationalist, anti-immigrant movement and the growing Muslim population in Germany. And they see as well the decline in interest in the Jewish past in Germany and in especially the Holocaust, as it comes to be seen more and more as a historical period of the past which that no longer meaningfully informs the present.

Appendix: Methodology and Sources

Anthropology, history, genealogy and journalism all share the same research conundrum: how to get trustworthy information from untrustworthy sources. Untrustworthy does not mean that the information sources are willfully dishonest, although they sometimes are, but that the information was most likely collected by individuals and organizations for reasons other than one's current research; that it was biased for political or religious or other reasons; that it represents only the interests of those holding power; was collected long ago and employed language and concepts no longer in use; was written down many years after it was first gathered; was written in a foreign language or dialect or obsolete script; mentions unknown people; uses obsolete place names; and so on.

How to get trustworthy information from these untrustworthy sources? The best way is to: (1) gather information from multiple sources and compare that information; (2) use sources written by individuals who were observers of the events they describe; and (3) use sources written in the native language of the people being described. Most importantly, accept the limitations of the information and resist the temptation to fill gaps with logical assumptions, analogous reasoning, or imagination. In gathering the information for this book, I have kept these principles in mind and have therefore gathered and combined information from eight types of sources.

1) Ethnography, including visits to communities and sites, observation and participant observation.
2) Interviews.
3) Memoirs.
4) Personal documents – letters, financial records, day books, address books, etc.
5) Genealogies compiled by myself and others.
6) Family histories compiled by myself and others.
7) Photographs and illustrations.
8) Official records and documents of governments, churches, and organizations including censuses; tax, property, voting records, and civil records; registry lists; deportation lists; and concentration and death

camp lists.
9) Primary publications – newspapers, periodicals, books, pamphlets.
10) Secondary sources – books, articles, websites

It is sadly ironic but also encouraging that we now have a rich and growing record of many of the Jewish German communities that disappeared during the Holocaust and even some that disappeared in earlier times. We benefit from that record because for the last thirty or so years, the study of Jewish German individuals, families and communities of the past has been something of an ever-expanding enterprise in Germany and elsewhere. This effort rests on the research skills of a diverse group of organizations and individuals including the Leo Baeck Institute in New York, Yad Vashem in Israel, Jewish genealogical services and internet sites, Jewish and Holocaust museums; the German government; professional and amateur researchers in the U.S. England, Israel and Germany; and Holocaust survivors and their children and grandchildren.

To my considerable benefit, this Jewish community history enterprise in Germany included a number of very active researchers studying several of the communities of interest to me, most importantly Uehlfeld, Adelsdorf, Burghaslach, Heddernheim, and Frankfurt. For the Middle Franconia district of northern Bavaria there is a group of researchers who every other year publish the results of their research in the online journal *Mesusa*, under the editorship until 2014 of the late Johannes Fleischmann. These local researchers play a key role in preserving Jewish history by finding and preserving and sharing documents, photographs and information. Another important source were Holocaust survivors who shared their personal knowledge of the communities or individuals of interest. Included here are people on the 1992 trip and my mother's friends and relatives who shared information over the years, even though neither they nor I had any idea what they said would one day inform this book.

The major reason we are able to learn about these Jewish communities is that the record of their existence and of the individuals who made up the communities usually survived the war. Germans were obsessive record keepers and many community records survive, although many others and especially earlier ones were lost in the many wars and fires that consumed the German states. Nearly all records of Jewish communities from the early 1700s on survived because the Nazis wanted to preserve registers of births, marriage, and deaths so as to be able to determine if people had Jewish ancestry and how much ancestry (number of Jewish grandparents) they had. The goal, of course, was to identify Jews so they could be eliminated. Some of this material is now available online but most remains stored in government offices and libraries and private collections. A small amount of material was also taken from Germany by Jews fleeing in the 1930s and some of this is available in family histories and family genealogies posted online or housed in archives.

Primary Sources

Adler, Elkan N. ed. (1987), *Jewish Travelers in the Middle Ages.* NY: Dover. Orig. pub. in 1930.

Azulai, Hayyim David Joseph (1997), *The Diaries of Ha'im Tosef David Azulai (Ma'gal tov' – The Good Journey).* Jerusalem: Bnei Issakhar Institute. Translated from the Hebrew and annotated by Benjamin Cymerman.

Bamberg State Archives. Translation of 'Annual Accounts of the Dachsbach Districts, Uehlfeld Districts, Real Estate Transactions of Neustadt District'. In the Friedrich R. Wollmershaeuser Collection. Leo Baeck Institute Archives, Center for Jewish History, New York.

Biographies. Projek Jüdisches Leben Frankfurt am Main. www.judisches-leben-frankfurt.de.

'Boycotting Activity in Neustadt am Aisch'. Shoah Resource Center, Yad Vashem. www.yadvashem.org.

Frankfurt, city directory 1935, 1938. Frankfurt: Jüdisches Museum der Stadt Frankfurt am Main.

Emanuel Loew Hopf Collection, 1820-1976. AR 4284. Leo Baeck Institute.

Glückel of Hameln. (1977). *The Memoirs of Glückel of Hameln.* NY: Schocken Books. Translated with notes by Marvin Lowenthal.

Gawronski, Hans. Personal communications with Irma Levinson and David Levinson, 1992-1993.

Haberkamm, Harmut. Personal communications with Irma Levinson and David Levinson, 1995-1999, 2012, 2014.

Henry Skirball Collection. Leo Baeck Institute Archives, Center for Jewish History, New York.

'History of the Volunteer Fire Brigade, Market Uehlfeld'. Feuerwehr Uehlfeld www.ff.uehlfeld.de/Geschi.html.

Johnson, Valerie. Personal communications with David Levinson, 1994-2001.

Kahn, Irwin. Personal communications with David Levinson and Irma Levinson, 1992-1994.

Karras, Steven, ed. (2009). *The Enemy I Knew.* 'Chapter 2. Jerry Bechhofer'; 'Chapter 16. Walter Reed'; 'Ch. 21. Fred Fields'. Zenith Press.

Kolbet, Christiane. (1994). Personal communication with Irma Levinson.

Lax, Margot. Personal communication with David Levinson, 2012.
Loewi, Isaac. (1831). 'Antrittsrede des Herrn Dr. Isaak Loewi, bei seiner Installation als Rabbiner zu Fuerth, gehalten am 21 Maerz 1831'. Fürth Druck: Zirndorfer. Leo Baeck Institute Library, Center for Jewish History.
'Markt Burghaslach'. www.alemmania.judaica.de.
'Markt Uehlfeld'. www.alemmania.judaica.de.
Menk, Lars. (2005). *A Dictionary of German-Jewish Surnames*. Bergenfield, NJ: Avotaynu.
Ortmeyer, Benjamin, ed. (1996). *Eyewitnesses Speak Out Against Denial*. Bonn: Marg. Wehle Witterschlick.
Reed, Walter. Personal communications with David Levinson and Irma Levinson, 1993 – 2003, 2012 – 2015.
Richarz, Monica, ed. (1991). *Jewish Life in Germany: Memoirs from three Centuries*. Bloomington: Indiana University Press. Translated from the German by Stella P. and Sidney Rosenfeld.
Ron, Baruch. (2010). 'Der Tag, an dem meine Schoah begann: Die Geschichte des Baruch Ron'. *Mesusa 7*.
Rosenfeld, Samson Wolf. (1819). *Die Israelitische Tempelhalle, Orde die neue Synagoge in Markt Uhlfeld, ihre Entstehung, Einrichtung, und Einweihung (The Jewish Temple Hall, or the new Synagogue in Market Uehlfeld, its Development, Establishment, and Inauguration)*.
Schmer, Karl. (n.d.). 'Juden in Uehlfeld: Vom warden und vergehender Uehlfelder Judengemeinde'. 2 vols. Unpublished manuscript, Uehlfeld, Germany.
Schwab, Josef. (n.d.). 'Erinnerungen aus Meinem Leber 1801-1900'. Unpublished manuscript. Leo Baeck Institute, Center for Jewish History. New York.
Smerin, Richard. (n.d.). 'Adelsdorf'. www.richardsmerin.com/cd_08_text.html
Skyte, Heinz and Thea Ruth Skyte. (c. 1995, 2006). 'Our Family'. Rijoresearch 2.0. www.rijohomepage.t-online.de.
Skyte, Thea. Personal communication with David Levinson, 1995.
State Archive Nuremberg: 19th Century Emigrants from Central Franconia to North America. Saginaw, Michigan: Saginaw Genealogical Society. www.rootsweb.ancestry.com.
Stolpersteine Frankfurt. (2015). Documentation - Josef, Rosa, Ferdinand Gruenewald and Lina Rindsberg. www.stolpersteine-frankfurt.de/dokumentation_en.html.
Tuchmann, Friedrich Carl. (1928). 'Stamnbaum und Chronik der Familie Tuchmann aus Ühlfeld Neustadt/Aisch'. www.geni.com.
Uehlfeld, town of. Civil and property records, 19th and 20th centuries. Uehlfeld, Geramny.

United States Holocaust Memorial Museum. www.resources.ushmm.org.
Yad Vashem. Database of Shoah Victims' Names. www.yadvashem.org.
Yondorf, Eric, trans. (2006). The 'Edict of June 10, 1813 Regarding the Status of Persons of Jewish Faith in the Kingdom of Bavaria'. Rijo Research 2.0. www.rijo.homepage.t-online.de.

Secondary Sources

Baader, Benjamin M. (2006). *Gender, Judaism, and Bourgeois Culture in Germany, 1800-1870.* Bloomington: Indiana University Press.
Bacigalupo, Italo. (1989). 'Ländliche Synagogen im Aischgrund'. IN *Steiflichter aud der Heimatgeschichte.* Geschichts – und Heimatverein Neustadt a. d. Aisch.
Bodemasnn, Y. Michal. (1996). *Jews, Germans, Memory: Reconstructions of Jewish Life in Germany.* Ann Arbor: University of Michigan Press.
Bookhagen, Rainer. (2002). *Die Evangelische Kinderpflege und die Innere Mission in der Zeit des Nationalszialisms: Rückzug in den Raum der Kirche. Band 2: 1937 to 1945.* Göttingen, Germany: Vandenhoeck & Ruprecht.
Cahnman, Werner. (1989). 'Village and Small Town Jews in Germany'. In *Germany Jewry: Its History and Sociology*, edited by Joseph Maier et al. New Brunswick, NJ: Transaction Books.
Costa, Marta D. et al. (2013). 'A substantial prehistoric European ancestry amongst Ashkenazi maternal lineages'. *Nature Communications* 4. 2543 doi: 10.1038/ncomms 3543.
Davis Randers-Pehrson, Justine (1999). *Germans and the Revolution of 1848-1849.* New German-American Studies/Neue Deutsch-Amerikanische Studien. New York: Peter Lang.
Elon, Amos (2002). *The Pity of It All: A History of the Jews in Germany, 1743-1933.* NY: Metropolitan Books.
Ehrmann, Hilmar Bruce. (1948). 'The Struggle for civil and religious administration in Bavaria in the first half of the nineteenth century as reflected in the writings of Rabbi Samson Wolf Rosenfeld'. Unpublished thesis. Leo Baeck Institute Library, Center for Jewish History.
Faludi, Christian, ed. (2013). *Die 'Juni-Aktion' 1938.* Frankfurt: Campus.
Fause, Gary C. (2005). *Erlangen: An American's History of a German Town.* Lanham, MD: The University Press of America.
Ferguson, Niall. (2015). *Kissinger: 1923 – 1968: The Idealist.* NY: Penguin.
Fischer, Stefanie. (2010). 'Clashing Gears: Jewish Cattle Dealers, Farmers, and Nazis in Conflict, 1926-35'. *Holocaust Studies: A Journal of Culture and History* 16 (1-2): 15-39.

Fleischmann, Johann. (1998). 'General History of Rural Jewish Communities in Aisch, Herzogenaurach, Ebrach, and Seebach'. *Mesusa* 1: 24 –36.

Fleischmann, Johann. (1998, 2000, 2002, 2004, 2006). 'Spuren Jüdischer Vergangenheit in Aisch, Aurach und Seebrach. Die jüdischen Friedhöfe von Zeckern, Walsdorf, Aschbach, Uehlfeld, Mühlhausen, Lisberg, Burghaslach and Reichmannsdorf'. *Mesusa* vols. 1, 2, 3, 4, 5.

Friedman, Jonathan C. (1998). *The Lion and the Star: Gentile-Jewish Relations in Three Hessian Communities, 1919-1945*. Lexington, KY: University of Kentucky Press.

Galliner, Paula. (1966-99). 'The History of the Jews of Baiersdorf'. AR 3015, Leo Baeck Institute.

Gay, Ruth. (1994). *The Jews of Germany: A Historical Portrait*. New Haven: Yale University Press.

Gellately, Robert. (2001). *Backing Hitler: Consent and Coercion in Nazi Germany*. New York and Oxford: Oxford University Press.

German National Tourist Board. (2014). *Germany for the Jewish Traveler*. www.germany.travel.

Gilbert, Martin. (1985). *The Holocaust: A History of the Jews of Europe During the Second World War*. New York: Henry Holt and Company.

Goldfarb, Michael. (2009). *Emancipation: How Liberating Europe's Jews from the Ghetto Led to Revolution and Renaissance*. New York: Simon & Schuster Paperbacks.

Goshen, Heike Z. (n.d.) 'Burghaslach'. In *Destroyed German Synagogues and Communities*. www.germanysynagoguies.com.

Haas, Hans-Christof. (2016). 'The "Israelite Temple Hall" in Uehlfeld as Prototype of a Reform Synagogue in the Kingdom of Bavaria'. In *Reform Judaism and Architecture*, edited by Andreas Brämer, Miko Przuystawik, and Harmen H. Thies. Petersberg: Michael Imhof, p. 131-146.

Harris, James F. (1994). *The People Speak! Anti-Semitism and Emancipation in Nineteenth-Century Bavaria*. Ann Arbor: University of Michigan Press.

Heim, Susanne. (2001). 'Emigration and Jewish Identity: An Enormous Heartbreak'.

Holocaust Studies: A Journal of Culture and History 10(1): 21-33.

Henry, Francis. (1984). *Victims and Neighbors: A Small Town in Nazi Germany Remembered*. South Hadley, MA: Bergin & Garvey.

Hübschmann, Ekkehard (2013). 'Jewish emigration to the free states of America in the 19th century'. Paper presented at the 33rd IAJGS International Conference on Jewish Genealogy, Boston, MA, Aug., 4-9, 2013.

Jochem, Gerhard. (2007). 'History of the Hops trade in Nuremberg'. www.rijo.homepage.t-online.de.

Kaplan, Marion A. (1991). *The Making of the Jewish Middle Class: Women, Family, and Identity, in Imperial Germany.* New York: Oxford University Press.

Kaplan, Marion, ed. (2005). *Jewish Daily Life in Germany, 1618- 1945.* NY: Oxford University Press.

Kober, Adolf. (1940). *Cologne.* Philadelphia: The Jewish Publication Society of America. Translated from the German by Solomon Grayzel.

Kochan, Lionel. (2004). *The Making of Western Jewry, 1600-1819.* New York: Springer.

Lowenstein, Steven M. (1981) 'Voluntary and involuntary limitation of fertility in nineteenth century Bavaria Jewry'. In *Modern Jewish Fertility*, edited by Paul Ritterband. Leiden: Brill Archive.

Mann, Vivian B. (1982). *Two Cities: Jewish Life in Frankfurt and Istanbul 1750-1870.* NY: The Jewish Museum.

McGregor, Neil. (2015). *Germany: Memories of a Nation.* NY: Knopf.

Meyer, Michael A. (1995). *Response to Modernity: A History of the Reform Movement in Judaism.* Detroit: Wayne State Univ. Press.

Miroslav, Marek. (2014). 'House of Hohenzollern'. www.genealogy.euweb.zz/hohz/hohenz 1, 2. Html.

Naumann-Götting, Inge. (2011). 'Das Hotel Kronprinz'. Weisbaden: Aktives Museum Spiegelgasse für Deutsch-Jüdische Geschichte.

Panayi, Panikos. (2014). *Ethnic Minorities in 19th and 20th Century Germany: Jews, Gypsies, Poles, Turks and Others.* NY: Routledge.

Paulus, Konrad, comp. (n.d.). 'Die Geschichte von Uehlfeld und Umgebung'. Uehlfeld.

Pressler, Mirjam, with Gerti Elias. (2011). *Treasures from the Attic: The Extraordinary Story of Anne Frank's Family.* New York: Doubleday. Translated from the German by Damion Searls.

Richarz, Monika. (1981). 'Emancipation and Continuity: German Jews in the Rural Economy'. In *Revolution and Evolution 1848 in German-Jewish History*, edited by Werner E. Mosse. Tubingen: J. C. Mohr.

Rieger, Susanne and Gerhard Jochem. (2015). 'Jewish Topography of Nuremberg'. www.rijoresearch.de.

Rose, Emily C. (2001). *Portraits of Our Past: Jews of the German Countryside.* Philadelphia: The Jewish Publication Society.

Schneeberger, Michael. (2012). 'Ein froher Schauer ergriff das Gemüth – Die Geschichte der Juden von Uehlfeld. Jüdische Landgemeinden in Bayern [31]'. In *Jüdisches Leben in Bayern München 26*. Jahrgang/Nr. 118/ Pessach 5772 – 4.2012.

Scheierz, Israel and Rudolf Sussmann. (1983). *Zeugnisse Jüdischer Vergangenheit in Unterfranken.* Bamberg: Bayerische Verlagsanstalt.

Shevitz, Amy. (2007). *Jewish Communities on the Ohio River: A History*. Lexington, KY: The University Press of Kentucky.
Skyte, Heinz and Thea Skyte. (2009). 'The History of the Jews of Baiersdorf'. www.rijo-research.de.
Skyte, Thea. (1995). 'The Jewish Community of Burghaslach'. *Stammbaum* 5: 22-26.
'Uehlfeld (Mittelfranken/Bayern). Aus der Geschichte jüdischen Gemeinden im duestschen Sprachraum. www.xn-judische-gemeinden-zzb.de.
Simons, Janet. (1997). 'Old wounds finally healing: German village welcomes Jews who escaped before WWII'. *Rocky Mountain News*, May 7, 1997. www.highbeam.com/doc/1G1-67660818.html
Spuren Jüdischer Vergangenheit in Adelsdorf. (1996). Erlangen: Gruner Druck.
Stern, Selma. (1950). *The Court Jew: A Contribution to the History of the Period of Absolutism in Europe*. Transaction Books.
Voigtländer, Nico and Hans-Joachim Voth. (2012). 'Persecution perpetuated: The Medieval origins of Anti-Semitic violence in Nazi Germany'. *The Quarterly Journal of Economics*, v. 127, no. 3. www.qje.oxfordjournals.org/content.
Wawrzyn, Heidemarie. (n.d.). 'Uehlfeld'. In *Destroyed German Synagogues and Communities*. www.germanysynagogies.com.
Werner, Klaus, Helga Krohn, and Christa Fischer. (1990). *Juden in Heddernheim*. Frankfurt: Jüdisches Museum der Stadt Frankfurt am Main.
Yronwode, Catherine. (2009). 'German Jewish Families in the Hops Trade in Franconia'. www.yronwode.com/kohn-erlanger-family.html.

Index

Adelsdorf, 32
Africa, 21
Aisch River Valley, 34
Anna, the Electress of Saxony and Brandenburg, 39
Ansbach, 34, 61
anthropological method, 1, 2, 4, 5
Ashkenazim, 19, 24
Augsburg, 20, 27
Austria, 27, 45, 76, 82, 115, 137

Baiersdorf, 38, 40, 44, 54, 61
Bamberg, 91, 102, 103
Bavaria, 9, 10, 27, 34, 36, 71, 72, 76 – 9, 81 – 6, 94, 103, 104, 134
Bayreuth, 27, 34, 44, 48, 61, 78
Belgium, 129
Belitz, 27
Berlin, 102, 121
Black Death, 27, 29
'blood libel', 26
Bohemia, 115
Brandenburg, 27, 34
Bremen, 117
Breslau, 27, 122
Burghaslach, 9, 33, 40, 53, 65, 70, 97- 9
burial societies, 66

cattle dealing, 67, 69 – 71, 103
Charlemagne, 20, 23
China, 21, 129
Cincinnati, 95
Cologne, 18 – 20, 26, 27
Congress of Vienna, 80, 117
Constantine, Emperor, 18
court Jews, 40, 41, 61, 114
Crusades, 25, 26
Cyprus, 137
Czechoslovakia, 129, 137
curia, 18

Dachsbach, 47, 111
Danube, 20
Danzig, 122
Dark Ages, 21
Denmark, 129
department stores, 105

'desecrating the host', 27
Dingfelder family, 67, 73, 103, 105, 110, 111, 135
disputes and conflict resolution, 63 - 5
DNA research, 19

Edict of Emancipation, 63, 73, 78, 79, 83–5, 96
education, 56, 57, 84 –7, 117, 118, 124
Einhorn, Rabbi David, 93, 94
emancipation, 73 –96, 100, 105, 117, 118
England, 27, 29, 122
Erlangan, 40
Ernst, Margrave Christian, 39, 40, 55
Evian Conference, 133

Final Solution, the, 130
Fourth Lateran Council, 26
France, 20, 21, 23, 27, 29, 82, 129
Franco-Prussian War, 110
Franconia, 9, 36, 37, 38, 40, 77, 78, 80, 134
Franconia, Middle, 34, 40, 42, 78, 106, 132, 134 - 6
Frank, Anne, 126
Frank, Otto, 126
Frankfurt am Main, 1, 27, 75, 77, 83, 102, 113 – 123, 135
Frankfurt on Hudson, 123
Franks and Frankish Kingdom, 20
Fürth, 9 – 11, 38, 88, 93, 102 - 4

Geiger, Rabbi Abraham, 88, 93
George, Margrave Frederick I, 39
German Confederation, 80
German Empire, 100
ghettos, 26, 27, 115 - 7
'Golden Age, The', 23, 24
Great Britain, 129, 133, 137
Gruenewald family, 119, 120, 123
guilds, 62, 118

Haberkamm, Helmet, 112
Hamburg, 27, 75, 117, 122

Hanover, 12
Hansa cities, 22
Hedernheim, 119
Hep! Hep! riots, 80
Hilders, 82, 83
Hirschau, 107
Hitler, Adolf, 129, 132, 134, 135
Höchstadt, 35
Holdheim, Rabbi Samuel, 88
Holocaust,1, 4, 17, 127– 137; displaced persons, 137; refugees, 132, 133; survivors, 137 (*see also* Hitler, Adolf;National Socialist German Workers' Party; Uehlfeld)
Holy Roman Empire, 11, 23, 80, 114
Hopf, Loeb, 104, 105
hops dealing, 71, 103 - 4
Hungary, 115, 129

Ibn Kohrdadbeh, 22
Islam, 25
Israelitische Gemeinde, 63
Italy, 18, 20, 21, 27, 114, 137

Jacobson, Israel, 88
Jewish-Christian/German relations, 12, 13, 15, 17, 25 – 7, 37, 41 - 4, 52, 58, 59, 82, 83, 90, 98, 106 – 111, 116, 118, 120, 121 (*see also* persecution of Jewish communities, protection)
Jewish communities and the Holocaust, memorialization of, 32, 33, 114, 128, 137
Jewish Germany, 110; assimilation of, 122– 6; community organization, 14, 15, 38, 50, 52, 63–6, 105, 113, 117, 120, 121, 124, 125; demography of, 7, 8, 15, 96, 120– 2, 137; distribution of, 7 – 9, 11, 102, 113; early settlement of, 18, 19; economics of,

37, 83, 84, 105, 119; foundational principles, 7 – 17; leadership of, 50, 63; marriage and family, 15, 38, 50, 52, 97; occupations 37, 60, 96, 102, 116 –8, 119; property ownership, 58 – 60; post-Holocaust, 137 – 140; taxation 37, 47, 48, 52, 57, 58; variation within, 14, 105, 120, 121, 124 – 6
Jewish Question, the, 129, 135
Judaism, organization of, 38, 50 – 4; practice of, 23 – 5, 38, 42 - 4, 50 – 3
Judaism, Neo-Orthodoxy, 114, 117, 121, 124
Judaism, Orthodoxy, 89, 93, 94, 117, 119, 121, 124
Judaism, Reform, 11, 54, 80, 88, 89, 91 – 4, 114, 117, 119, 121, 124
Judaism, Reform, United States, 94
Jüdischen Gemeinde, 63
Jüdischer Frauenbund, 119, 126

Kabbalah, 43
Karl, Margrave George Frederick, 42 –5, 55
Kestler, Walter, 130, 131
Khazars, 19
Kindertransport, 133
Kley, Edward, 88
Kristallnacht, 127, 130, 136, 138

Leipzig, 122
Levinson family archive, 2, 3
Lichtenau, 85 - 7
Lithuania, 27, 91, 108, 129, 137
Loewi, Rabbi Isaac, 92, 93
Lubeck, 117
Ludwig II, King of Bavaria, 93, 97
Luther, Martin, 42

Magdeburg, 20
Main River, 20
Mainz, 17, 18, 20, 23, 26, 27
Matrikel, 73
Mendelssohn, Moses, 88, 91
Mediterranean, eastern, 18
Merseburg, 20
Metz, 20
Meuse, 20
mischlenge, 130, 131
money lending, 26, 63
Moselle, 20
Munich, 102, 104, 122, 134
Musgiller, George, 111, 112, 127

Napoleon, 77
National Socialist German Workers' Party (NSDAP, Nazi Party), 9, 105, 129–131, 133 - 6
Netherlands, the, 27, 129
Neustadt an der Aisch, 39
nobility, German, 34
Nuremberg, 9 - 11, 27, 39, 44, 77, 83, 102–5, 120, 122, 134, 135; International Military Tribunal, 135; Laws of 1935, 122, 129

Oppenheimer family, 40, 114, 121
Ostjuden, 125, 126

Palestine, 122, 129, 137
persecution of Jewish communities, 9, 20, 26, 27, 39, 41, 42, 46, 80, 100, 101, 114, 120(see also Holocaust)
Philanthropin School, 117, 124
Poland,14, 27 - 9 45, 46, 108, 115, 129, 137
Pope Gregory, 20
Portugal, 26, 27, 114
Prague, 20, 26
'protection', 12, 13, 46 – 8
Prussia, 34, 76, 77, 81, 114, 117

rabbinate, 28, 54
Radhanites, 22, 23
Ratisbon, 20
Reed, Walter, 75, 112
Regensberg, 26
Revolution of 1848, 76, 81, 82, 89
Rhine River and Valley, 18 – 20, Rindsberg family, 33, 35, 36, 66, 67, 70, 73, 75, 76, 78, 79, 94, 95, 97 – 100, 109 – 2, 119, 120, 123, 127, 130, 131
Roman Empire, 18, 19
Roma, 135
Romania, 129, 137
Roosevelt, Franklin Delano, 133
Rosenfeld, Rabbi Samson Wolf, 79, 80, 84, 85, 90 - 3
Rosenthal, Simon, 85, 86
Rothchild family, 40, 114, 116, 117, 121
Russia, 45, 108, 129, 137

Samson Solomon, 40
Saxony, 27
Seckel, Moses, 61
Selz, Rabbi Chaim, 93

Shum cities, 23, 25
social control, 64, 65
South America, 129
Spain, 26, 27, 114
Speyer, 20, 23, 26
Speyer family, 121
Streicher, Julius, 135
Sturm family, 33, 97 - 9
surnames, Jewish, 73 -75
Switzerland, 129

textile industry, 71
Theodoric the Great, 20
Thirty Years' War, 35, 39
trading, Jewish, 20, 21, 25, 26, 29, 60 - 2, 67, 69, 96, 102 (*see also* cattle dealing, hops dealing, textile industry)
Treaty of Versailles, 100
Troyes, 18, 24
Tuchman family, 75
Turkey, 115

Uehlfeld, 9, 31 –49, 58-61, 64, 65, 67, 68, 71, 72, 73, 75, 78, 83–5, 90, 97 – 100, 102–6, 108, 112, 127, 130, 131; commemoration of Jewish community, 32, 110; during the Nazi era, 134–6; fires, 35, 109; Jewish cemetery, 31, 32, 55, 56, 66; Jewish demography and settlement, 35, 36, 38, 39, 44 – 6; rabbis and rabbinate, 42 – 44, 54, 55; synagogue, 55, 91 –3, 109, 110
Ukraine, 129
United States, immigration to 14, 38, 95, 96, 105, 122, 123, 129, 137
Upper Palatinate, 36

van Berg, Veit, 35
Verdun, 20

Weimer Republic, 100, 102
Wise, Rabbi Isaac Mayer, 94
World War I, 100, 110, 120, 125
World War II, 117
Worms, 18, 20, 23, 26
Würzberg, 20, 27, 80

Yiddish, 28, 29, 56, 57, 70, 91, 108, 109, 126

Zionism, 19, 121, 124, 126
Zschokke, Heinrich, 91